# Cannabis Recipes

And (2 in 1)

# Connoisseurs' Guide

Other books by: (Jasselin) Joseph G. Asselin
All published by Jasselin.com
Publishing since 1979

**English books**
A Pat on Your Back
Justice Now
When Justice is Death
Cannabis Recipes and
(2 in 1) Connoisseurs' Guide

**French books**
Un Monde à Revers
Quand Justice est la Mort
Penser Succès
Une Tape dans le Dos
Réinventons notre Vie
**Livres de recettes** 1985
Les Recettes de la ferme (4 saisons) Tome 1
Les Recettes de la ferme (Pot-au-feu) Tome 2

Publisher : www.jasselin.com

# Cannabis Recipes

## And (2 in 1)

# Connoisseur's Guide

Published by; Jasselin.com (publishing since 1979)

The Guide to Become a Cannabis Connoisseur    3

Cannabis Recipes and (2 in 1) Connoisseurs' Guide
By (Jasselin) Joseph G. Asselin
Publisher: Jasselin.com
Publishing since 1979
All rights reserved. 2019 © Library of Congress, U.S. copyright

Legal deposits to: Canadian National Library and
Quebec National Library. (Fourth trimester 2019)

Printed at the Point of Sale.
ISBN (Export Trade Paperback) 978-1-927652-21-3

ISBN numeric (eBook) 978-1-927652-20-6

Typesetting and designs by Jasselin.com

Readapted version, Translated from
The original French version: copyright in France:
Recettes de Cannabis et (2 dans 1) Guide du Connaisseur

French version Copyright © 2019, Joseph G. Asselin, France 45B61C8

All the recipes in this book are worldwide captured and inspired by friends while traveling all around the world, and then reconstituted on my stove top.

So, if there is any food elaboration resemblance to your own recipes, it might be purely coincidental.

Jasselin.com—publisher

Publisher : www.jasselin.com

# What's in this connoisseur's guide (2 in 1)

## And cannabis recipes book

Essential information to safely consume and prepare foods and beverages, compatible with the process of assimilation and absorption, through the capricious digestive system.

Safe and economical ways to make your own ingestion.

Other, faster, but slightly more expensive ways, as found at dispensaries.

Selected recipes, chosen for their fat and sugar content (just enough, but not too much) for not to load the stomach; which could interfere with assimilation.

Essential information to prevent and correct, in the event of overdosage disorders, red eyes, or drug testing prevention.

A significant diversity of teas to create, which is by far the best and most cost-effective of the millennial means of consuming for "HIGH" or health…

And so practical tables, for metric conversions and food substitutions.

And all of this is focused on health, above all!

The star recipe is: Angels' Cream!

**READ THIS: (in addition)**

This cannabis cookbook can become a simple cookbook, without cannabis; just remove the cannabis ingredient in the recipe. You can do the same with your own favorite recipes. But, there are basic to follow, and how to do it, mention in this book, tricks for transforming your recipes.

Why is the index there, at the beginning of the book?

Because, it's very practical, if you have the numeric version: you press ctrl + click and there is the page you want.

Otherwise, by reading the index, you have a contain fast view of your practical BOOK!

# Index

# Introduction

The purpose of this book is to expose to you, a wide range of processes for extracting the maximum intensity and saving for your money. But above all, to give you enough information and elaborated tools to consume safely.

Yes, it is a cookbook, because primarily, consuming cannabis in your food or beverages is better for your health than smoking by breathing in the burnt resin; it's as bad as those who smoke nicotine asphalted tobacco. And, not to mention all other chemicals that manufacturers hide in it, to create dependency. But usually, tobacco smokers are the same people who smoke marijuana, but the worse of it, is the eventual price to pay back, will be so desolate…

Each of us mind their own business we should say, yes, but that's the reason which has stimulated me to do intensive research to get people to consume rather than smoke. To many of my friends and family members suffered martyrdom, before death. So, I would like to help smokers for living longer, a healthier life!

This book is also an implement to demystify the misunderstanding, that surrounds the ingestion of cannabis. All of us has at one time enjoyed a cold beer with friends, well, not many people know that hops, used in beers, is a variety of cannabis's family. And the same goes for hemp, which you probably have in your cereals, with which ropes and clothing have also been made for thousands of years.

I've long heard people look up at those who were smoking marijuana, but what about eating it or drinking it? Same thing, prejudices have entered the mind of scrupulous people and does not seem to pass out.

No one believed me, never did anyone want to believe that they had ever used cannabis while drinking beer. But after checking on the internet, some of them, the less scrupulous admitted with embarrassment that they had done research. However, none wanted to clarify their research, for not to admit their misunderstandings and especially not to feel guilty for having indirectly consumed a derivative of cannabis...

But things are changing and it seems that we are approaching the end of the world, so everything is going too fast now, and in every way...

So, enjoy the greenish revolution! And think above all, about your well-being.

**READ THIS: (in addition)**

This cannabis cookbook can become a simple cookbook, without cannabis; just remove the cannabis ingredient in the recipe. You can do the same with your own favorite recipes. But, there are basic to follow, by transforming your recipes.

# CHAPTER one

## The Same Rights for All of Us

It's all about the kind of consumer or producer, who wants to transform his or her precious stimulants by themselves. This book is for all levels of followers, otherwise we would have to say: "go to the dispensaries, they have shelf finished products, ready to use." But for those who are serious about their choices and want to combine the pleasure of doing everything themselves, this book is also and especially for them.

The monetary side is also in question. Those who produce their 4 plans as permitted in Canada, because they cannot afford to buy oils or tinctures in dispensaries, they also have the right to treat themselves and have fun... The laws are different in all states and countries where cannabis is legal. Canada is one of the first countries to legalize cannabis for medical and recreational purposes.

Before legalization, everything was like a free-for-all to consumers. The black market was the way to obtain their junk, full of carcinogenic pesticides, from Mexico or Colombia.

There was no instruction, no labels, no directions, and certainly not a wide range of enticing choices. Now, with legalization sweeping the world, edibles have gone from easy to get and better quality controlled too, plus competitive prices.

For those who want to make their own edible products at home, the field is vast, the limits are cooking competences, the available budget and the pleasure of creation.

# Read this first

This book is either first or foremost a cookbook because that is what cannabis users want. That's why you have the table of contents at the beginning. You have to have the digital version, you just have to click on it by pressing control (ctrl click) and your recipe appears.

Then, it is specially set up to inform you about what can happen to you as a cannabis user.

So, for the summary of its contents, read the table of contents first, but, for general information you will find them at the end. The reason is that when you often open your cookbook, you don't want to stand in your hands on items that you will only see once in a while or when a problem arises.

This cookbook is for all levels of consumers: beginners, regulars and those looking for improvements in their extraction processes. And do not forget the rights to consume too, for those who have no money to go to dispensaries sometimes too far from their homes and those who make their own culture.

## THE DISPENSARY

On your first visit to the dispensary, you may be a little intimidated by what has finally become legal after such a long prohibition and prejudice about cannabis. But, if you already know the questions you want to ask, then you'll look like a pro … at last!

# The Questions the Pros Use

The people who will serve you, have been trained to help you with good advice, so you just have to question them. Before you ask questions, you must first know what you want and which purpose…
Please state if it is for a health problem or for entertainment.

**Questions:**
- **What are your favorite products for entertainment? Or for health.**
- **What are customers' favorite products and why?**
- **What products do you recommend?**
- **How intense is the product?**
- **What is the taste and smell of the product?**
- **How do I use the product?**
- **When the first effects of the "High" and for how long it will last?**

The most important thing is to know what you want. Maybe it's just a curious visit, before a next purchase, or to tempt yourself without getting an arm twisted.

# THE DIFFERENCE BETWEEN THE CBD AND THE THC

CBD and THC are both cannabinoids, active chemicals that act on the body's receptors: (nervous system, organs, immune system). The noticeable difference is that tetrahydrocannabinol (THC) is psychoactive, while cannabidiol (CBD) does not make you STONE, is non-psychoactive and poses no health hazard.

# CBD, versus THC: What are the differences?

Cannabis is composed of several hundred molecules, cannabinoids, and all endowed with their specific properties. THC, for tetrahydrocannabinol, is the active substance known for its psychotropic effects. It is the THC that helps to change the state of consciousness of the follower, making it high "euphoric." When the choice is for a recreational product, it is a cannabis product rich in THC that is mentioned.

The cannabidiol CBC is another cannabis molecule with a different purpose, such as calming the nervous system and countering the effects of THC to limit its properties to a certain level. CBD can delay the effects of THC and increase it tenfold, but by limiting the risk of anxiety and anxiety attacks sometimes generated by active THC consumption. In other words, as already mentioned, CBD does not make STONE, it has no psychotropic effects. It is chosen for its therapeutic virtues.

## CBD: Therapeutic Virtues:

Because of its psychoactive effects, THC is still considered as a drug in most countries, even in countries where cannabis is legalized. THC tends to be addictive, and especially because of psychoactive stresses on the body. As for CBD, it produces the same therapeutic opposite.

The race in research increasingly demonstrates that cannabidiol CBD has emancipated and potentially revolutionary therapeutic virtues. CBD has an anti-inflammatory properties, helping to combat anxiety and depression, calming the symptoms of epilepsy and multiple sclerosis, and working against certain psychotic disorders such as schizophrenia, and more. Other studies suggest that with high concentrations, CBD would act as an inhibitor in the proliferation of tumor cells from certain cancers, and that after a heart attack, it would reduce the risk of artery necrosis. Research in the therapeutic field suggests a great opportunity. However, studies to date have shown that CBD is not toxic and does not create dependence; "unlike THC."

## How does our system digest cannabis?
Our digestive system is a device that ages faster than we do as a whole, because we are abusing it.

## Digestion:
A few details to specify the importance of balancing your way of consuming to reap the most benefits.

Research has shown that THC is more effectively assimilated if it has been dissolved in fats, oils or alcohol. When fats or oils are ingested, the liver receives a signal to secrete bile, which is then concentrated in the gallbladder and then ejected into the duodenum.

Bile is an alkaline liquid that helps emulsify digestion and fat absorption. Cannabis stimulates the flow of bile to some extent. But if cannabis resins are induced in the system without the presence of fat, there may not be enough secreted bile, to carry out their complete assimilation. But in the end, only a percentage of the resins will be assimilated. When food is injected into the stomach, hydrochloric acid and enzymes begin digestion.

And, when the contents of the stomach become liquefied, small amounts are ejected into the duodenum at intervals of about 20 seconds until a certain amount accumulates there. Then, a very small amount of fat can be absorbed directly into the bloodstream through the intestinal capillaries, and, bile begins to emulsify the scattered fats into tiny droplets in the liquid, making certain fatty acids finally soluble. And then, more of these fatty acids can be assimilated into the duodenum.

What is not assimilated will be digested in the small intestine by pancreatic lipase (an enzyme). All stomach emptying operations can take anywhere from one to four hours.

## Alcohol:
Only a few substances like water, alcohol, and some drugs are absorbed directly through this organ. Alcohol is fairly quickly absorbed by the lining of the stomach and will act as a vehicle to transport into the system other substances, with which it is associated.

## Sugar:
Because honey and other sugars are quickly absorbed into the blood stream by the intestinal capillaries, they can also be used, to some extent, as a vehicle to facilitate assimilation. But since THC does not dissolve in sugars, the degree of absorption is rather limited.

The signal for the stomach, to slow down the process of ejecting its contents into the duodenum is caused by a hormone (inter gastric). This hormone is released from the intestinal lining into sugars or fats in the small intestine. If too much sugar is present, fats containing active resins will be retained longer in the stomach.

Following this research, the conclusion is that the presence of a little sugar in alcohol or in an oil-based confectionery can facilitate the assimilation of THC. However, too much sugar can interfere with fat digestion and decrease the effects of THC and CBD.

Also, too many foods ingested will dilute the potential of THC and CBD. So a little food is better than a busy stomach and, most important, choosing the right kind of food as in this book, is preferable…

Publisher : www.jasselin.com

# Drink Water, It's Essential to Assimilate!

A dehydrated person, mis absorbs all strains of cannabis and the effects could also be very different with more fluid in the stomach. Our whole body would be floating better! And in addition, to confirm it further; According to the institute of medicine, it is recommended to drink at least 10 glasses of water per day. But a Florida television channel reported that while most people know very well, that water is the way to go, while nearly 75% of the U.S. population does not have 10 cups per day prescribed by the American Medical Institute. This means, in general health terms, that most Americans operate in a chronic state of dehydration.

## Water is also vital with cannabis:

Water is vital and also when we use cannabis, because our system needs liquid to function and assimilate better.

"60% of our body is made up of water, 75% of our muscles, 85% of our brain.

## WATER: it's like the oil of a machine."

The Americans, "reported by a New York newspaper" would buy more soda than water, the news may not be new, but health officials insist on the importance of good hydration.

**"People just think that when they start to get a little weakness or have a headache, they need to eat something, but more often than not, they just need to drink."**

According to a credible report: "Water is necessary for the body to digest and absorb vitamins and nutrients. It is also the key to proper digestion. If our body has water, it detoxifies the liver and kidneys and carries the waste to a normal cycle.

'It's a bit like the planet "A" earth, which is a huge body. The normal cycle of the earth receives water, filters it by removing nutrients from the arable layer and then releases the excess filtered into the rivers; if the planet "A" lacks water, everything dries up and we die-of-thirst…'

We can take a test on our own, if our urine gets dark, it is because we are at a certain degree of dehydration. The urine should be clear."

## Lack of water causes of disease:

Over time, not drinking enough water can lead to many medical complications, such as fatigue, joint pain and weight gain, headaches, ulcers, high blood pressure and kidney disease.

On the other hand, much of our consumption of liquids, other than water, can have adverse effects on our health, such as caffeine-containing beverages and diuretics.

"In the U.S., people tend to drink a lot of slightly dehydrated beverages as well."

For those who can't stand the taste of water, there is a wide variety of fruits and vegetables that can be mixed with distilled water; often, people do not like water because they have the sensitivity to capture chlorine products and superfluous undesirable minerals in the cities' treated water and even from artesian wells…

This is an explicit summary of several articles that I had in hand for a long time and I was only waiting for the opportunity to share them with you… The sources are diverse, but credible, after verification…

# Beer and Hops

Hops, derived from a variety of cannabis, has been used for beer seasoning for a long time. It contains a substance called,

Publisher : www.jasselin.com

lupulin which is chemically linked to low THC traces. It tends to act as a light sedative and it is the hops that give the beer its bitter taste and relaxing side until sometimes drowsy.

New varieties of plant crossings are emerging, they will certainly find themselves in the beer of tomorrow.

One of the past difficulties was to extract enough cannabis resin from hop fruit. Also, cannabis resin that is not water soluble, does not dissolve in beer because beer is too low in alcohol.

The beer alcohol content, even if higher, would be insufficient to dissolve the resins.

Introducing alcohol to beer during brewing at the brewery would stop the fermentation process. For those who would like a more well-stocked beer, the quickest way is to add a few drops of tincture or concentrated oil, directly into the bottle. Old countries have been doing this for a long time…

# SMOKING it or eating it?

Smoking the grass or eating it through pleasant recipes? It is a healthy choice that must be made according to one's own priorities…

Who could say, if it is reasonable to inhale smoke, which will damage the lungs for sure? Hot tarred ash is among the highest causes of respiratory diseases, causing excruciating death. But today, hopefully, since the legalization of cannabis there is a range of new ways to use cannabis.

When choosing health and longevity, edibles are a wise choice…

However, easygoing often presents us with the path that motivates our choices. It's quicker to roll a joint and share it with friends than to spend an hour cooking and another hour preparing the tastings. Yes OK! But we have only one throat and only one respiratory system and only one life; if we don't protect it, then who's going to protect it? What was true yesterday is no longer true, with all the new products on the market like the tinctures you can add to any food or beverage, everything has become instantaneous.

Smokers and those who prefer to eat or drink edibles do so for the same reasons; the search for pleasure and the desire to share socially with friends.

## Effects:

Usually, when marijuana is consumed reasonably, there are no known side effects. However when consumed in excessive amounts, it can cause a listless feeling and bloodshot red eyes the next day and persistent headaches.

The only advantage when cannabis is smoked is that the effect is almost instantaneous. Some grasses (herbs) may take five minutes or will then light up quickly, but usually the highs are usually felt right away.

## Joints and 50% Loss

Joints are not economical and burns a part of your reserve in smoke in the air. During the whole time a joint is lit, it burns grass and only a small portion of that smoke actually enters your lungs. Unless you smoke it all the time, hoping you don't choke.

The other advantage than smokers prioritize is that even though "high" usually lasts only one to two hours, they can light on another joint and take a few puffs to quickly recover the "high" before a pronounced decline. Unfortunately, in this case, smokers do not think about the negative consequences of the respiratory system. The note will be salty, the day when the lungs could no longer take it... My brother was OK, and three months later he died.

# "High": The Waiting Time

When ingested in food, cannabis is slow to get on, 30 minutes to an hour and a half before the first symptoms of High are felt. (Except with tinctures and beverages.) And then, the euphoric state continues to increase. But the appreciable advantage is that the High can last, from 4 to 8 hours and sometimes even longer, up to 12 hours. This flat state (High) can be very useful to a person who wants to stay in a place where it is impossible to hide the smoke and without mentioning the smell of cannabis. It's no longer the way to sneak into toilet cages, to grab a quick tuft; especially during an intermission at the theater or during an indoor show.

Although ingested cannabis can take about 90 minutes for the first effects, most of the recipes in this book are created to work faster. The new beverages are among those that activate quite quickly the first perceptible buzz, in fifteen minutes. Research has shown that the psychopharmacological effects of ingested cannabis are very different from those of smoked material.

## The Highs faster and faster

All new products on the market, since the cannabis legalization, according to numerous discoveries on THC and CBD, are paving the way for new hallucinogenic or medicinal applications.

In all respects, it is more beneficial for the wallet and health, to ingest cannabis in good little treats, first because drinking or eating cannabis, provides more hallucinogenic effects than smoking a joint or vaping.

Therefore, joint or ingestion, one should not take the risk of driving a vehicle or performing any task that would require accurate perception, judgment and response of skill. The social side, to roll a joint, with a small group of friends, has its good memorable side, but, cooking a meal and enjoy it with friends with the pleasure of sharing good special foods, has its very entertaining side too.

But remember to take a taxi, first for the risk to have a stupid accident or the getting a salted fine if the police arrest you, and worst, suspended driving license.

And a final advantage of smoking is that it is almost impossible to overdosage. By smoking, the smoker may choke on smoke or set fire to his bed and alert neighbors who will call the fire department. But, eating non-stop while waiting for the first aerobatic effects to arrive could offer a high unchecked and lose consciousness from 12 to 36 hours, according to friends lived experiences. It's all about common sense and prudence, as much as driving a car as it is about taking stimulants for fun.

It is recommended to start with light dosages and increase to higher aerobatic highs as experience allows… Each person has different reactions, depending on their ability to digest and react to cannabis products.

The physical and chemical nature of cannabis and how it is absorbed into the digestive system must be taken into account.

# CANNABIS SOLUBILITY

The active substance in cannabis is not directly soluble in water; it is soluble in oils, fats and alcohols. This has been known for thousands of years. However there are light varieties like hemp and hops that have been processed to be soluble with liquids.

This was true before cannabis became legal; but everything is changing, as if Mr. CANNABIS had just come out of his shell. Producers and researchers are in a frenzy!

As for solubility in water, this dilemma was solved a long time ago for different strains derived from marijuana (cannabis). Hemp, the same product with which clothes are made with it, is a kind of cannabis, but that doesn't mean you could chew your blonde's panties to get a high. Hops are also from the same family as marijuana, a lighter plant than marijuana, which brewers have been adding to their beer for a long time…

Recipes known from India and other hash-consuming civilizations, used to have ganja sautéed with ghee (clarified butter) before combining with the other ingredients in the recipe; they were getting more benefits. When hemp products were available for almost nothing, it was fashionable to simply boil the product to drink it with pleasure, but the high was never coming, but, on the other hand, they had fun in the feasts.

## Choosing the Right Cannabis Dishes

Our usual food is not the kind of food, which goes hand in hand with cannabis, for reaching the pinnacle "High". To get a good relationship, "cannabis and light meals," you should choose small snacks, not too sweet and not too greasy. On the other hand, it is recommended, according to studies in this area, that dishes should be little oily and even a little sweet; apparently this would facilitate the assimilation of cannabis. And also, not to mention alcohol, which is an accelerator that goes directly to the blood. More on this is mentioned, and more explicitly, a little further?

## Cannabis Stimulates Appetite

Ingestion of cannabis stimulates appetite. Weed smokers often have a small craving, but when ingested, cannabis really opens the appetite, depending on the variety consumed. So when you use cannabis, you'll know why you need to eat treats. If the craving persists, it is best to settle for a small snack. Otherwise, a little hot water with a tablespoon of honey should soothe your cravings.

As already mentioned, too much food in the stomach, digesting cannabis, could throw down your high very fast. Especially if you have stomach problems. Too much food in the belly will surely interfere when you try to experience euphoria.

## HIDING THE TASTE

Among old and modern cannabis recipes, preparations are overwhelmingly trying to cover the taste of marijuana, which many people find unpleasant.

The Indian Majoon is a typical example of this approach. It's a sweet and spicy confection with cinnamon, cloves, cardamom, nutmeg or other condiments, and all this to mask the flavor of hemp.

# CHAPTER 2

## DO EVERYTHING, by yourself
More information on our website: www.mari-juana-blog.com

## Products, to save time and money

It's better to make your own (cannabutter) cannabis butter, cannabis oil (canna oil), canna milk (Canna-Milk, coconut oil). More and more, finished products are pouring into the market and it's just starting out in the race. But not everyone can afford to buy finished products such as tinctures, waxes and concentrated oils; that's why this book gives you so many details, the health way and how: DO EVERYTHING?

# LECITHINE an indispensable food addition

Lecithin increases the absorption of cannabinoids into our cells membranes and accelerates the process of assimilation, especially when added to cannabis and coconut oil.

Since assimilation is more receptive with added lecithin and therefore faster, the dosage of food may be lighter, thus also more cost-effective; and nevertheless, while focusing on our health.

Don't easily believe everything said, it's easy to find out online, because you know that everyone tries to pass their salad. It is a bit like the bad reputation in the past, on all strains of cannabis, such as hops, hemp and marijuana. The fundamental reason was obvious, cannabis was too perfect, so the No. 1 enemy of our capitalist systems... Hey, they might be saying to themselves: "We're not going to allow people to take care of themselves!"

## Lecithin:

Adding lecithin to your general diet can be a great way to increase nutrient absorption and release cell membranes hardened by past questionable diets.

Lecithin:
- Lecithin helps improve our immune system.
- Offers better protection against the invasion of viruses, and bacteria.
- Helps eliminate cholesterol, triglycerides and harmful fats.
- It prevents hardening of the arteries and strokes.
- Makes it easier to transmit nerve impulses into the brain, improves memory and helps brain cells emancipate.
- Lecithin also serves as a solvent that facilitates the fastest distribution of cannabis into the bloodstream.
- And the same goes for all that is ingested, lecithin plays a major role in the absorption of nutrients in cells.

Suggested amount of lecithin:
- It is always better to add your lecithin to the recipe itself, instead of mixing it in your infused products after decarboxylation (to avoid separation).
- If you want to mix it in your Canna coconut oil or your canna butter, then it is best to use liquid lecithin.

For each cup of canna or canna butter oil, add:
- 1 cup canna coconut oil, after decarboxylation.

- **1 tablespoon sunflower lecithin.**

# Why is coconut oil recommended?
Its saturated fat quantity is doubly superior to other oils.

## Why is coconut oil the best?

It should be noted that coconut oil is the most widely used medium in desserts and beverages for its high saturated fat content of about 50%, compared to other oils with less than 20% to 30%. And coconut oil is particularly renowned for facilitating assimilation through the demanding assimilation elements of our digestive system… And it goes well with the lecithin emollient properties…

# How to prepare food at home

It's made easy, if you keep in mind that every time a recipe contains an oil, or regular butter, then you mix your dosage of canna oils, or your cannabis-infused canna butter, with your basic ingredient.

Canna butter, oils, concentrates, glycerin, alcohol, fats and even milk are potential cannabinoid extraction drivers. So all we have to do is make food to your liking.

## Make Edibles With Concentrates

Concentrates are an instant way to add a dosage of cannabis infusion to any edible recipes you create at home. The advantage of concentrates is the display of detailed dosages, % THC and CBD intensity and also, detailed aroma and flavor.

## Add grass to a meal

You have control over the power you want to consume, and if a minor is seated with you, he will not have the oil drop to concentrate that the law forbids him to have.

Knowing beforehand the percentage of THC and CBD, helps you to prevent that the recipes to be consumed ultimately, will come out too low or too strong in intensity.

In addition, concentrates allow you to respect each other's choice, and to dosage foods accurately, depending on the individual degree of assimilation for each of your guests. Whether it's a few drops of concentrates, in a drink or a teaspoon in a vegan coconut soup, it's much easier to get a similar result every time you cook.

### Taste and Scent

The terpenes are natural plant compounds included in almost all plants including cannabis. They are also included in the aroma you choose: aroma of lavender, pines, diesel, citrus or pepper, etc.

This is interesting for home edible lovers, as concentrates add flavor to marijuana foods.

# ZIP Bag Decarboxylation

**There are many ways for decarboxylation on the internet.**

The decarb techniques preferences, are a vacuum technic in a zip bag and the Mason jars way, why?

- **You don't burn anything like decarb it in the oven.**

Moisture in any parts of cannabis contains a juice that also has nutritional and active values, which would evaporate in drying.

In its natural envelope, the whole plant protects its precious value, the resin, from possible parasites intrusions, and when we consume it, the whole plant has properties for us that our body has yet to discover.

One of the advantages of a vacuum in a zip bag is that your home, you and the neighbors will not smell cannabis in full nose…

The main advantage, apart from the scent, is that all the precious values, will be kept inside the vacuum envelope (zip bag) immersed in water or in a Mason jar.

After decarb, another and not the least of the benefits is that you let your slow cooker do injection with your oil without worrying about it, for a good 8 hours, while you are at work. This is because your vacuum bag is submerged in low boiling water (water displacement) and the water simmering over medium heat will not exceed 200 F (100 C). Then you will never burn your cannabis by risking reaching 250 F. (especially, that the ovens are not accurate with 10 degrees less or more); making it a 20-degree variant.

## The Easy Way

You can also choose not to bother about decarb and put everything in the zip bag and let the decarb processing by the same time with the injection of your coco oil (especially because coco oil is high in saturated fat). But if you use alcohols, it's safer to do it with a stainless steel container.

After whatever decarb your choice, you then prepare your oil recipe by simmering all day:

- **2 tablespoons of coconut oil, for each gram of cannabis.**

The other preferred decarboxylation process is the Mason jar, but there is still a danger of broken glass. So, with a stainless steel container, the size of Mason jar, that solves the problem. Be serious with your health, never use aluminum containers or aluminum cooking pots, for cooking; because residues extracted from overheated aluminum will remain in your body forever and eventually cause diseases. Do make a search on the internet, about this, to convince you.

To explain all the controversial basics regarding the ideal of decarboxylation processes, a complete book would be needed. The main direction of whatever process to put into practice is, first of all, to know where, and how much "HIGH" you want to ride. However, if it's CBD to improve your well-being, everything is different. Even if this book contains many details necessary for any fan of cannabis uses, it is safely obligatory to know how far we want to go through our experiences…

Therefore, you can find more information on our WEB website: www.mari-juana-blog.com

Even if the site is in development because of the exorbitant time required to develop this book:

- **In French first.**
- **And then in English, about a month later (December 2019), because it's still in correction.**

For other readings by the same author: www.jasselin.com


# A little precision:

Why there are so many ways to deal with decarboxylation?

- **You aim for what THC or CBD?**
- **Which variety you have in hand?**

In any direction you choose, it will have an influence on the temperature and time you will apply for decarboxylation. And there are many varieties in the market with what you can get your need. But for those who don't like to bother with decarboxylation, you put everything in a zip bag and let it be done by itself; Especially if you use coconut oil or alcohol or glycerin…

Many recipes in this book to do so…

# CHAPTER 3

## HOW TO MAKE YOUR Basics Materials

### Don't go any further until you've de-oxidized your cooking pots!

Do not go any further before you have de-oxidized all your cooking pots for cannabis and then they will have to be used only for your CANNABIS. Those who don't have money for expensive pots, flea markets overflow of varieties.
WARNING: Aluminum pots never de-oxidize and it's a health crime to cook anything with aluminum, because aluminum residues will stay in your system forever and when your body has too much, diseases will appear.

If you don't have a double boiler, use a smaller pot in a larger saucepan in which you will put the water. And put the double boiler on your shopping list and don't forget, please, never use this double boiler for anything other than cannabis. And above all, never wash it again with water and soap. To be sure that you don't have oxidation in your recipes. New or used, before using it, you should treat your double boiler or cannabis cooking pots with cooking oil and salt, that you'll heat and wipe off. This process is to de-oxidize your pots. Otherwise you'll get black matter that you won't like… When finished, clean your pots with cooking oil again, wipe off with paper towels and store. And do the same before you use it, not to induce dust in your magic portion of cannabis. Who likes dust and cooked flies-dirt-droppings?

# THE GHEE SACRÉ

Ghee in India is still called (SACRED GHEE), but for us, the basis of preparation is the butter. Our butter, once called "poor fat," has the disadvantage of separating at room temperature; while prepared in ghee by the transformation of "isomerization," it acquires the advantage of being able to be kept for a long time without separating at room temperature. Or, even better, in the cold, with low temperature, it will keep even longer, and above all, will not give this brownish color when cooking. You may use it for eggs cooking with no brown stuff around…

## GHEE PREPARATION

Many recipes specify butter, but you have the choice to use what you have on hand. Isomerized butter (ghee) has the advantage of not separating when it is not refrigerated or when heated over the fire. Our butter produces a kind of scramble that annoys when mixed with our favorite dishes. Cleverly prepared, our "ghee" can be stored for a long time without refrigeration and even longer when only slightly refrigerated.

## Method to Make Your Ghee

A first method is to heat a pound of fresh butter, or more, in a pot, not too hot, and not boiling over high heat, but to the point where the butter produces a scramble that you remove with a spoon. The more foam you remove from the surface, the purer your butter becomes ghee. After this first success, you can consider bigger recipes. But be careful not to burn your butter by heating it too much, otherwise it will be "burnt butter" that will spoil the taste of your pot, but will only be burnt butter. The ghee has a light caramel buttery taste and is dark gold.
You're worth it!

# The decarboxylation
## (The Magic Thing)

To get the maximum intensity extracted from your cannabis, the magic trick is to proceed, first, by decarboxylation of which here are the basics to succeed:

# Cannabis herb decarboxylation

### Why decarboxylate?

Heat, to some degree, exposes cannabis cannabinoids to decarboxylation, a process of chemical modification of the structure is then modified so that the body assimilates differently, the original product, through the channel of blood circulation. The simplification of this current synthesis serves, at least, as a starting point to go further…
The next step is to explain the main reason why decarboxylation of weed grass is important and how to do it safely at home.

## Activates the effects

The action of "decarboxylating" cannabis is the process that causes a chemical reaction, in order to eliminate by evaporation, to a certain degree of heat, oxygen and carbon molecules out of THCA, and CBDA and various other cannabinoids, which are evaporated, which one found in the natural cannabis plant, to finally get the desired properties, such as THC and CBD.

Processed cannabinoids are chemical compounds that attribute cannabis to its attractive health and entertainment effects. The use of decarboxylation removes the direct chemical link, which prevents the acid cannabinoid unnecessarily entering the bloodstream.

This is why the consumption of fresh marijuana directly from the plant, without decarboxylation, does not produce psychoactive effects.

The treatment by decarboxylation of edible products is therefore one of the most important aspects to obtain the desired properties.

Decarboxylation allows various targeted cannabinoids to penetrate more freely into the bloodstream, through the mouth, stomach and intestines. Active cannabinoids must pass through the digestive system to be exposed to the metabolic processes of the liver; this is probably the speculative reason that the effects take longer to come when consuming food, versus smoking. This explanation is simplified, so as not to lead to long scientific specifications.

## What could change its chemical structure

If you live in a state or country like Canada, where marijuana is used for recreational and medical purposes, the specific state, provincial or country regulator is responsible for

Publisher : www.jasselin.com

protecting the health of their citizens in relation to cannabis use, which is why they impose stringent safety tests, such as:

The origin of the product, so as not to allow products infected with pesticides or harmful mixtures from the black market from Mexico and Colombia, which use forbidden and carcinogenic pesticides.

Then, for those who really care about their health, they can be sure that aging products whom may be infected with mold are being tested before the product reaches the consumer, etc.

## Cannabinoid concentrations

Details such as THCA and THC on a label can easily confuse inexperienced consumers or those who used to eat on the pesticide-sprayed black market.

The hasty changes in the market and the influx of many products do not bring more knowledge to the consumer.

## More about decarboxylation

The user in general, who has limited experience, only wants to learn about the fundamentals. He wants to extract the maximum intensity, from raw marijuana in the process, not easy to understand, the decarboxylation. The simplified explanation for decarboxylation is that decarboxylation transforms THCA into THC, CBDA into CBD and also activates natural terpenes and flavonoids, present in cannabis.

The result depends mainly on the freshness, quality and concentrations of cannabinoids in raw plant material, as well as various environmental factors combined with the cannabis decarboxylation process. As for terpenes, they give cannabis its flavor and smell, which some do not like…

THCA (A is for acid) does not produce a "High" effect and its neurological interaction has been shown to be different from that of THC, while CBDA and CBD, although both are non-psychoactive and express and mimic their effects differently in the neurological level.

## Prelude to decarboxylation

The decarboxylation of your herb, also called decarb, is essential if you want the biological intensity, on different levels, available forms of THC, CBD. Other various fewer preferred cannabinoids are being available too by that process. The decarboxylated cannabis herb, in that initial stage, can then be used for infusing with:

- Various vegetable oils, which can be easily added instantly to various recipes such as beverages, salad dressings, spice blends, delicacies, and even syrups, all of which can produce a high intensity, depending on the dosage induced in the recipes. And this, as much for therapeutics as for leisure.
- Butters, such as canna butter, are in demand in many recipes and mix.
- Fats as coconut oil can replace butter too.
- Alcohol, used mainly for high-intensity tinctures, or oral atomizers, mainly used in the health field and to those who can afford it.

It should be noted that coconut oil is the most widely used medium in desserts and beverages for its high saturated fat content of about 50%, compared to other oils with less than 20%.

Why oils, fats, butter, glycerin and alcohol? Simply because the heated resin (a kind of tar) does not mix with water (unless the water is mixed with a high 70% to 90% alcohol content.

## For More Details

If not used as the perfect plant, various cannabis-related varieties, such as hemp (for clothing), hops (for beer) and marijuana, would have normally grown wild in the rough normal environmental conditions. Like anything that grows around us, and without worrying about it, they would still produce flowers and die in a natural cycle.

But researchers have discovered the benefits, but was kept in secret by our capitalist systems, for the purpose of feeding us with chemical pills and enriching multinationals, at our expenses…

## Smoking! hey!

That's why smoking or vaping marijuana has been the methods perpetuated for millennia, that was the only but illegal way to use marijuana. According to old documents, a Chinese emperor used "hemp" marijuana 5,000 years ago…

And, simply because the mystery was simplified by the modern consumer researchers, who were tired of sacrificing years of their life for smoke; (a major cause of death after suffering from lung cancer). And, finally, the research is providing an intermediate solution to smoking.

## The Decarboxylation

While heat is the transition agent in the decarboxylation process, the chemical transformation process works at some degree of stable heat. Decarboxylation not only helps activate cannabinoids, but if performed at too high temperatures, it could over activate the product, or if too low, lessen the end result of decarboxylation, thus completely altering the benefits of the expected effect.

The temperature, between 225 F—235 F (110 C-112 C) for 45 minutes to 1 hour, seem to be working well.

**Avertissement :**

La quantité d'huile ou de beurre ou de teinture au cannabis indiquée dans ces recettes est une suggestion très vague, car il est impossible de savoir le % d'intensité que vous avez en main. La quantité réelle que vous devez utiliser doit être modifiée en fonction de la force de vos produits de cannabis et de la puissance désirée en tenant compte aussi de la capacité d'absorption individuelle de chacun. Doser des aliments maison peut être obligeant. Le meilleur moyen de tester votre résultante est donc de commencer avec une portion réduite pour découvrir votre tolérance, dans ce cas une cuillerée à thé, puis d'attendre une à deux heures, et alors, décider en connaissance de cause d'aller plus « HIGH ». Dosez toujours avec sureté et écoutez votre corps et ne conduisez jamais sous l'influence du cannabis.

# CHAPTER 4

## YOUR EXPERIENCE starts here:

- Determine the dosage for infusion
- The amount of cannabis needed
- Freely grounded (by hand) for easier decarboxylation
- In a flat oven container (baking sheet)
- Spread your cannabis well ventilated for drying

First, you need to measure your desired amount of cannabis for decarboxylation. (Start little by little)

This varies depending on the user and the expected dosage you want to inject after decarboxylation, in butter, grease, oil or coconut oil, and maybe even a honey syrup or tinctures.

Make sure it is finely ground and place it in a baking sheet that can go to the oven.

Spread evenly in the container for ventilation.

Preheat the oven to 230 F (110 C)

Then place the container in the oven, without cover and (make sure that the oven temperature never get higher or lower than 230 F - 235 F [110 C], because the ovens have a variance of 10 degrees more or minus).

After 20 minutes, stir your grass a little quickly, to ventilate and ensure equal decarboxylation (at this stage, you can cover loosely with aluminum foil).

Approaching one hour, remove from the oven and let stand. Wait a minute, before removing your success from the plate.

Now, your chemically processed and softened cannabis can be used appropriately to infuse the medium of your choice, as stated earlier in this article…

## Make your own experience

Let's do your own experience! Because everything will depend on the cannabis material you have in hand: its freshness, its age, its origin, its variety and finally, the need aimed for…

## Make your canna butter (cannabutter)

Before you do anything, there are steps to follow and there are so many ways to transform your magic herb, but here are the most experienced and known easy ones. If you cook small recipes from time to time, you don't have to do a lot of decarboxylation. The following canna butter recipe includes a different and fast process that includes a kind of decarboxylation and injection at the same time.

## Cannabutter (canna butter)

Canna butter is one of the most suggested "mediums" ingredients in most foods and snack recipes. Cana butter can also be prepared with seeds. But, to be infused, everything has to go through a process of decarboxylation, otherwise you will have only raw grass with a little more effects than eating a salad. However if you boil it in your spaghetti sauce, it is certain that everyone will at least laugh for almost nothing, so if you have flat jokes, it's time to pass them along that lunch…

# How to make Cannabutter (beginner)

With this easy-to-make and fast canna butter recipe, your edibles will be quicker to prepare. However, it is not the procedure to remove the maximum intensity of THC and CBD for your money. But ideal for the beginner.

**Ingredients:**

- **4 grams (1/8 ounce) of cannabis**
- **1 stick = ¼ of a pound of butter (125 ml)**
- **6 cups of water (1 1/2 L)**

Cook:

Put (1/8) ounce 4 grams of cannabis in a grinder (mixer) and turn it into a not too fine texture. (Double if you want more canna butters.)

To begin slowly, you may choose a medium THC intensity for the strain you'll be using, as higher THC levels will give a more potent butter. (But any part of the plant can give something.)

Then pour 6 cups of water into a pot and heat to the point of simmering (do not boil).

Add the butter stick (125 ml) and your ground cannabis in water, slowly, while the butter is melting.

As the butter melts and you smell yet, the fresh smell of cannabinoids invading the room, let it simmer.

While simmering stir occasionally, for at least an hour, be sure it would never boil.

The longer you heat the cannabis, the more intense the cannabinoids will be extracted; but no more than two hours.

**Warning:** you do not want to let the water reach its boiling point. If cannabis is cooked to a boiling temperature, cannabinoids will actually be evaporated and the butter will lose its effectiveness and intensity.

After about 1 1/2 hours 1 3/4, or less if you feel that your first experience satisfies you.

Remove from heat and let it cool down for a few minutes. Prepare the strainer in which you will spread the etamine to filter your magic liquid.

Put the strainer on a plastic container, large enough to hold your precious stock and not too high for it to fit in your refrigerator.

Always use a strainer to support the etamine, do not take the risk of tying it with an elastic around the plastic container. (As someone does do on the internet.)

While it is still warm then slowly pour the contents of the cooking pot over the etamine to be filtered.

Drain the precious butter, which looks more like oil, until the last drop off, to get the most out of it.

Wipe down with the back of a spoon to harvest even more, but don't throw away anything, either the oily water, or the cotton to filter (etamine) and its precious stock still good, nor your empty cooking pot, all of which will go to the refrigerator together.

Later, in another operation, all the residues will be used to make teas, coffees, soups or other beverages.

## Phew! What a deal!

Remove the etamine and keep it in the cooking pot with all the utensils (so as not to lose anything of the precious juice). In the meantime, make yourself a cup of tea or coffee and rinse the strainer with a good first drink that you will begin to feel within fifteen to twenty minutes.

The last drops collected, put your plastic container in the refrigerator and let stand for 5 or 6 hours to let the butter harden and separate from the water.

In the refrigerator, the canna butter will slowly separate from the water and solidify as it rises and floats above the water to form a layer of greenish butter, as if suspended over the water.

Five (5) hours over, your success is obvious, take out your plastic dish and see the result.

Also take out your first cooking pot and make a small bag with the etamine and its contents, and tie it with the cooking rope and leave it in its cooking pot (to receive the water from the plastic container, which is under the butter) then:

Make small holes in the butter, on the edge of the plastic container, to pour out the water and let it go into your first cooking pot, where also is your small bag full of good stock.

Scrape the butter off and refrigerate in a smaller airtight container. If you ever want to keep it for a long time, then fill it with water to prevent oxygen from aging it (or developing mold on it).

Now you have edible marijuana to cook with.

## TO FINISH:

Bring your first cooking pot to a boil with your small bag in it and simmer while stirring for 10–20 minutes, also rinse your plastic dish, remove your small bag and press it to drain the last drop.

Keep this liquid in the fridge and experiment with your herbal life, coffee, soup and treat yourself.

Thanks to all these little tricks, you'll get your money's worth and have fun with your friends.

# Why coconut oil (No. 1)

Coconut oil has become one of the most popular superfoods on the market. Coconut oil is a saturated oil composed mainly of fatty acids (lauric acid) with medium bonds, at 50%, compared to olive oil first pressure which is 30% saturated fat. And other vegetable oils, around 20%. Coconut oil has been associated with many medical benefits for its antioxidant properties, preventing bone loss and a marked acceleration of wound healing time. Coconut oil with cannabis makes it a magic oil, it is so commonly used that it is added to almost everything. It is the best oil to be associated with decarboxylation (after it's done) to obtain the highest activated resin intensity of THC and CBD, which has been extracted from.

## Benefits of Coconut Oil Canna

According to assiduous researchers, it is now, of course, unanimously acknowledged, that the benefits of coconut oil are incomparable, compared to other oils, for a maximum link with cannabis. Because coconut oil is rich in fatty acids, it can create a powerful binding agent for cannabinoids.

Comparing it to other oils that contain only 20% saturated fat, cannabis and coconut oil are literally a perfect alliance in the union: cannabis/coconut oil.

It should be noted, however, if we mention only intensity, that today's tinctures made with alcohol, can reach a concentration of intensity of almost 90 to 100%, depending on the process and materials used in alcohol-soluble extraction.

# Make your coconut oil canna

This magic oil is the most used in whatever the recipe and for various medications.

**Ingredients:**
- **1/2 oz (15 g) Cannabis (get quality buds)**
- **1 cup (250 ml) coconut oil (organic is best)**

**Cook:**
Spread several double of etamine and place your buds evenly on the center.

Crumble them by hand to make them more penetrating by hot oil.

Fold the opposite ends to trap your buds and make them a kind of soaking bag.

Tie up your bag of buds with kitchen string. Leave it free without tightening the buds, to let the bag expand into the bottom of the cooking pot.

Fill the bottom of a double boiler (double bath) with a few centimeters (3 inches) of water in the bottom cooking pot. Place the second on top and heat to a gentle boil. (Simmer only, not boil to a big broth.)

If you don't have a double boiler, use a pan and smaller pot that you will put in.

Add the cup of coconut oil to the top cooking pot and let it melt and add your kind of sachet (small bag) of buds into the top cooking pot, in the oil.

Add about 1 cup of water, just enough to cover the sachet of your buds that you have just placed into your top cooking pot.

Watch the heat, simmer, but never bring to a boil.

Simmer for about 1.5 hours. When the mixture has turned green, remove and store the bag and let your liquid cool.

Once cooled enough, the mixture should form two distinct layers, water at the bottom and oil hardened at the top. Just make a few holes in the oil and let the water drain off. (Always keep your cooking items, as there are still plenty of products soaked in it, to be recovered for your beverages.)

Store in a glass container and it's done.


And, because there's magic in that water that some get rid of, as well as in the residue in your little bag. You can boil it all and when you needed to add it into anything you like, liquid or solid.


how:

Once cooled, you can remove your oil hardened enough to remove it with a spatula. Then turn your double boiler over the stove and start the process again to get the most out of your money. Repeat the process again and keep the liquid for your coffees or teas and the like.

But don't forget to identify your Mason jars with enough precision to use them efficiently later. And use this experience for your future achievements...

## Where? Use coconut-canna oil.

For a little more information, coconut butter is mainly used in desserts, snacks and some beverages. But the main feature of coconut oil is its concentrated saturated fat content which is superior to other oils used for the most important step to extract the most intensity of your money in THC and CBD. Before decarboxylation, the raw product is THCA and CBDA (A for acid), but to extract the active resin, the material must be softened by a constant and chemical heat, heat-transformed heat and then be induced, either from alcohol or fat, oil, butter, to finally be soluble with liquids and food. Since coconut oil is the most concentrated in saturated fat, it remains the preferred. But let's not disdain alcohol.

## Make your Cana oil

Although canna oil is widely used in hot, cold desserts and beverages, tinctures are so easy that markets will soon be flooded with these extraordinary products.

Make cannabis oil with basic ingredients.

**Ingredients:**
- **1 to 1 1/2 ounces marijuana (15 g) ornamental or finely ground buds**

- **28 oz (875 ml) of extra-virgin olive oil, cold pressure, or your choice. (If you prefer, use peanut oil because it has no taste.)**

**Cook:**
Bring your oil to simmer in a saucepan, and turn down the heat to low, just before boiling. (It should never boil.)

Add 1 to 1 1/2 ounces (30 g to 45 g) finely ground cannabis and mix well.

Keep an eye on it constantly, make sure the cannabis doesn't boil, simmer between 1 1/2 and 2 hours.

When the buds are transformed, by this kind of decarboxylation, after about 1.5 to 2 hours, remove from the heat.

Pass your canna oil in a very fine sieve or etamine and once well filtered, store in a jar to preserve your magic canna oil mixture.

Many recipes require either canna oil, canna butter or cannabis tinctures and also honey infused with cannabis tinctures or coconut oil.

Store the canna oil jar in a dark place or in the refrigerator and properly identify the kind of oil, for not to mix them with your other oils or butters of different strengths of intensity and qualities.

Check the intensity, as this oil may be as strong as some tinctures, except that it does not contain alcohol. Be careful in the dosage of your coffee, and do not drive until you are at work. Use a few drops in your morning coffee, as this oil will open your senses.

Talk to your boss before, because if you work in creation, he had to agree, if he is a little awake to the modern reality…

# Make your canna milk (canna-Milk)
Necessary in several recipes on the web.

**Ingredients:**

- 1 liter of whole milk, or fatty milk, or coconut milk, or vegetable almond milk.
- 25 grams of your best marijuana: "tops."

**Cook:**

If you don't have a double boiler, use a pan, and a smaller pot.

Pour a few centimeters of water into the medium pan and bring the water to simmer over medium heat, in a gentle boil.

In another smaller stainless steel bowl, combine your 25 g of cannabis "tops, flower, buds" with your liter of milk and start whipping them together, slowly and evenly.

Reduce the boiling at low in the pan, so that the liquid keeps simmering lightly.

Place the top bowl so that the bottom of the bowl touches the hot water inside the pan or the bottom bowl. This will prevent your milk from curdling at a stabilized temperature.

Keep the heat low and cook milk and marijuana slowly to prevent THC from being ruined.

Stir occasionally to keep the mixture blending.

Cook Cannamilk for 30 minutes or for 2 to 3 hours, depending on the desired intensity you want.

Once ready, filter the mixture through an etamine, pressing with a spoon to get off the last drop.

Keep your Cannamilk in the refrigerator to inject in the recipes to come. You may have enough canna milk for your morning coffee at work…

For a larger quantity, double or triple the ingredients.

# Canna tinctures

**Tinctures products:**

Publisher : www.jasselin.com

Cannabis lovers will surely tell you that tinctures are the pinnacle of an instant and fluid means, to ingest its dosage… Liquid cannabis was one of the most popular ways to use cannabis before it was made illegal in the United States in 1937. Looking back in time, American doctors frequently prescribed medicinal cannabis tinctures to their patients, for almost everything that had made them sick.

In the states where cannabis is now legal, tinctures remain a popular medical option for those who can't or don't want to smoke or vaporize anymore.

You can make cannabis tinctures by sinking a cannabis flower in alcohol or glycerin. One advantage of tinctures is that they are:

- **incredibly discreet.**
- **Act quickly.**
- **They have little or no smell.**
- **And are easy to hide on yourself.**
- **And offer easy dosage control, up to taste.**

In addition, tinctures, concentrated oil and beverages offered now in the market, are considered one of the safest ways to use marijuana; mainly because they create no general threat to health and especially to the lungs. The other appreciated benefit is the speed of the early effects; within fifteen minutes and the High is not far away…

## Too many processes flood the net.
# MY FAVORITE:

Alcohol and glycerin:

1. Submerge and let the cannabis soak in alcohol, 1 inch (3 cm) higher than the cannabis, in a Mason jar for (5) days.

2. After five days, put 3 inches (7.5 cm) of water in a saucepan and fold a washcloth in 4 and arrange it under the Mason jar to make a thermal layer; and dip your pot in it, the lid loosened and heat to a boil and simmer for 20 to 40 minutes. (A little smell out of it, when you lose the cover.)

3. Let it cool down and store the alcoholic liquid in a larger Mason jar and set aside.

4. The same process (1) is repeated with distilled water (only), boiling for 10 minutes. After 10 minutes, put the liquid into your first Mason jar containing alcohol.

5. The same process (4) is repeated, but with glycerin.

6. After five minutes in the heat, stir together after rinsing all your utensils with a little boiling distilled water, but keep the water. And at the end you boil it all together.

And if you don't like alcohol, then boil until the alcohol evaporates before the water. (The alcohol evaporates at a lower temperature than water.)

And if the water bothers you, let it boil until evaporated... But the ideal is to keep everything without boiling too much and do not evaporate this liquid so versatile.

Filter well and spoil yourself.

You can separate this recipe into different forces (intensity) for different fusions with food and liquids. If you keep the alcohol, the speed of the "HIGH" will surprise you, because alcohol is assimilated true the stomach membranes rapidly...

# Mason Jar and bad smell

For those who are used to making their own canning, the Mason pot method will not be new.

My friend Paul was an adept of the canning way. His cold room in the basement was twice larger than his wardrobe. Every fall, he made his canned tomatoes and the like with at least 6 dozen Mason jars and he never had any broken pots or cracked.

But if you completely dip the pot of boiling water:

- **Never fill the jar completely, to allow expansion (one inch of the lid).**
- **Never put a cold pot directly in boiling water.**

Let it simmer for as long as you want, as the water never rises hotter than 220 F (106 C), so nothing will burn, but an hour is reasonable.

Some prefer the oven to 220 F (106 C) for 40 minutes of decarboxylation.

Or the method in the slow cooker or double boiler, with a little water in the bottom, but:

- **If the pot is not completely submerged in water, you use a slow cooker with the lid tight, but at first, after 15 minutes, loosen to ventilate and tighten. So the scent won't be too widespread.**

Finally, whatever the method of decarboxylation, you let it rest a little and insert your coconut oil and your cannabis:

- **2 tablespoons for every gram of cannabis.**

Then the method of the double boiler, or slow cooker (if you don't have a double boiler, see details at the end of the recipe for Cream of the Angels.

Then simmer before going to work and when back, everything will be ready…

# THE RECIPES
## Start HERE

**Renowned recipes from all over the world, some of which come from farmers.**

## warning:
The amount of oil or butter or cannabis tinctures indicated in these recipes is a very vague suggestion, as it is impossible to know the % of cannabis intensity you have on hand. The actual amount you need to use must be modified according to the strength of your cannabis products and the desired potency. Also, take into account the individual absorption capacity of each of your guest. Dosing homemade food can be obliging. The best way to test your result is to start with a small portion to discover your tolerance, in this case a teaspoon, then wait one to two hours, and then decide knowingly to go over "HIGH." Always use a safe dosage and listen to your body and never drive under the influence of cannabis.

# CHAPTER 5

Cannabis recipes adapted to make it flow well into our digestive system!

# THE SOUP

## Onions-canna soup

### Ingredients:
- 4 or 6 large, minced onions
- 1/2 to 1 ounce finely sifted marijuana (15–30 g)
- 4 tablespoons flour (48 g)

### Cook:
In a saucepan, sauté 4 or 6 large sliced onions in a generous portion of oil or butter. When the onions are almost cooked, but before starting to brownish, stir in 1/2 to 1 ounce of finely granulated marijuana.

(This portion of the recipe is depending on what you have in hand.)

Continue to sauté until the onions begin to get brown and remove the pan from the heat. Then sprinkle on the onions 4 tablespoons of flour and mix well.

Cover the pan and put it back on the stove, over low heat, for about five minutes and stir every few minutes.

Then, in a separate pot, heat a pint of water (568 ml) and transfer all your onion juice into this hot water.

Rinse the pan well with a little water and return this precious juice to the soup pot.

(Remember that the fats at the bottom of the pan contain a large part of THC and CBD. In addition, the oil will help with assimilation).

Add seasonings as you choose and simmer for 30 minutes.

**Seasonings for soup:**
- **Wine, cognac or brandy**
- **Sour cream**
- **Parmesan cheese**
- **Paprika...**
- **Or seasonings for onion soup**

Add any seasoning (depending on your taste).

Add a little wine, cognac or brandy.

Serve with a topping of sour cream, Parmesan cheese, paprika or onion soup seasonings.

Mix well before serving, so that everyone receives an equal portion of what is in the bottom and the delicious liquid on top.

The extraction of THC and CBD properties were carried out through oil and fat and alcoholic ingredients, without having to go through decarboxylation anteriorly.

This recipe is special, the taste of the herb becomes integrated with the onions. The sour cream adds more fat to help with assimilation and alcohol also helps, through the membranes of the stomach...

This soup is an ideal basic example for creating your own soup model. Instead of the onion substitute or add:
- **Mushrooms**

- **Asparagus**
- **Cream 35%**
- **Your choice of spices**
- **Choice of wine more full-bodied**

To apply your own variations to your recipes, for example, use mushrooms, asparagus or other things that come to your mind to try; instead of sour cream, use 35% cream. And the choice of spices is innumerable…

Take notes, they may be used for the ingredients variations for your next soup creation.

# Canna Chicken and Noodle Soup

**Against the common cold**

Chicken soups are favorites especially in the cold season of colds and flu and adding cannabis makes it an ideal prevention remedy and even treatment…

**Ingredients:**
- **1/2 cup chopped onions (125 g)**
- **1/2 cup chopped celery (125 g)**
- **1/2 pound minced cooked chicken breast (225 g) or to treat colds, substitute for chicken gizzards, liver and hearts and add lime or lemon.**
- **5 ounces vegetable stock (150 ml)**
- **60 ounces chicken broth (2 L)**
- **2 teaspoons canna butter (cannabutter) (10 g)**
- **1 tablespoon salted butter (15 g)**
- **1 1/2 cups egg noodles (375 g)**
- **1/2 teaspoon dried basil (7 g)**
- **Salt and pepper (to your liking)**
- **1/2 teaspoon dried oregano (7 g)**
- **1/2 cup chopped carrots (125 g)**

- **1/4 cup peas (65 g)**
- **1 cup sliced carrots (250 g)**

**Cook:**

Canna butter can be substituted with canna oil.

Using canna butter mixed with salted butter, cook onions and celery for about 3 to 5 minutes.

Make sure you never boil the butter and risk burning it and hold it over medium heat by mixing regularly.

Add chicken and vegetable broth and stir actively again.

Add noodles, basil, salt and pepper, oregano, carrots and peas.

If you use a tincture or want to increase the dosage using a tincture, add it here. If it's for the common cold, add (65 ml) 1/4 cup of Angel Cream.

Then add the chicken broth.

Bring the soup to a boil and immediately turn down the heat.

Simmer for about 22 minutes, watching carefully.

When simmering, compensate for evaporation with half water and chicken broth.

You can double the ingredients to help get rid of the cold or flu.

And a cup of Angel Cream could also confuse your symptoms…

About 6 servings

# Cannabis Tomato and Cheese Soup

**Tomato soup with melted and grilled cheese is a family delight. That's what makes it one of the favorite soups with cannabis.**

Ingredients:

- 1 medium chopped onion
- 4 large tomatoes
- 10 - 15 small chopped carrots
- 2 celery stalks, chopped
- 1 large can of tomato sauce
- 1 cube of chicken broth, or beef or vegetable
- 1 tablespoon chopped oregano (15 g)
- 2 tablespoons chopped fresh basil (30 g)
- 3 tablespoons canna butter (45 g) mixed with regular butter
- 3 tablespoons salted plain butter (45 g)
- 2 garlic cloves, grated
- 200 ml whipping cream (4/5 cup)
- Add salt and pepper if necessary.

**Cook:**

From a medium to low heat, melt the regular butter mixed with the canna butter in a large pot and add the onions, tomatoes, carrots and celery and simmer for about 10 minutes. (Salted butter is preferable because it can heat more without getting brownish.)

Add tomato sauce, chicken broth cubes, oregano, basil and garlic and simmer for another 12 to 15 minutes.

Then pour into a blender and let it mix slowly, adding the whipped cream and mix until uniform.

Transfer your soup back into your cooking pot and let it heat slowly, without boiling, until hot.

Remove from the heat and add ingredients to your liking by stirring, such as more tomato past, lecithin or a little Angel Cream...

About 10 servings to enjoy.

# Chicken canna dumpling soup

A thick, creamy chicken soup in which the canna enhances the flavor.

Ingredients for soup:
- 4 cups chicken broth (1 L)
- 1 cup water (250 ml)
- Seasonings:
- 2 tablespoons salted butter (30 g)
- 2 tablespoons poultry seasoning (30 g)
- 1 teaspoon onion powder (5 g)
- 1 teaspoon garlic powder (5 g)
- 1 teaspoon sea salt (5 g)
- 1 teaspoon dried parsley (5 g)
- 1 teaspoon dried basil (5 g)
- 1/2 teaspoon black pepper (3 g)
- Chicken and vegetables:
- 1 pound cooked skinless chicken breast (450 g)
- 2 cups of peas (450 g)
- 2 cups of carrots (450 g)
- In a separate bowl
- 1 cup all-purpose flour (115 g)
- 3 cups milk (750 ml)

**Cook:**
First, cook the chicken.

In a large pot, add chicken broth, water, regular butter and all seasonings and bring the soup to a boil.

Cut the cooked chicken breast into bite-size pieces and add it to the soup. Cover and continue cooking over medium heat for about 7 to 10 minutes.

In a separate bowl, combine flour and milk until smooth.

Slowly add the mixture to the soup with all the vegetables and cover.

Cook for another 10 minutes and start making the meatballs.

**Ingredients for dumplings**
- **1 1/4 cups flour (145 g)**
- **1 tablespoon baking powder (15 g)**
- **2 teaspoons sugar (10 g)**
- **1/2 teaspoon salt (3 g)**
- **2 tablespoons canna butter (30 g)**
- **2/3 cup milk (150 ml)**
- **2 tablespoons chopped parsley or dill (30 g)**

**Let's cook the dumplings:**
In a large bowl, combine flour, baking powder (baking powder), sugar and salt.

Add the canna butter and mix well and add the milk and mix again until the dough softens and forms a balloon.

Make dumplings with a tablespoon and slowly add them to the soup one by one.

At the end, to thicken the soup, if necessary, add more flour mixed with milk.

Cover and reduce heat to simmer for about 12–15 minutes.

And serve!

**NOTE: dosage**

We have to notice you that you have to be prudent, especially if you are a beginner.

The dosage of all recipes should be adjusted when brewing canna butter, especially if you are cooking with tinctures that you can add to your recipes to increase their potency.

Be careful with the dosage, start little by little and increase according to your own absorption capacity, which could be different for each of your guests and measure individually according to their digestive system. Some may be sick from a portion that is too large.

Soups, teas, coffees with cannabis can provide high effects quite fast compared to other food products. READ THIS:

**(in addition)**

This cannabis cookbook can become a simple cookbook, without cannabis; just remove the cannabis ingredient in the recipe. You can do the same with your own favorite recipes. But, there are basic to follow, by transforming your recipes.

# CHAPTER 6

# ENTRIES AND Coffe Brake

## Polish Asparagus Canna

Ingredients:
- 3 lbs of fresh asparagus (1 kilo-360 g) or 2 (bags) of 10 oz (284 g) of frozen asparagus tips.
- 2 tbsp minced onions (25 g)
- 1/2 cup butter (125 g)
- 2 tsp canna butter (10 g)
- 1 cup breadcrumbs (250 g)
- 2 tsp dried basil or tarragon (10 g)
- 1/3 cup lemon juice (75 ml)
- 1 tsp salt (5 ml)
- 1/2 tsp pepper (2 g)

Cook:
Place asparagus tips in a covered saucepan containing about 1/2 Po of boiling water (1.2 cm).

Cover and simmer until tender and crisp, about 10 minutes.

In a small frying pan, sauté onions lightly in butter.

Add breadcrumbs, seasonings and lightly brownish. Add and stir in lemon juice, salt and pepper and mix with melting canna butter.

Arrange drained asparagus on a hot plate and top with breadcrumb mixture.
Serves 6 to 8.

# CHINESE asparagus Canna

**Ingredients:**
- 36 asparagus tips
- 1/4 cup butter (50 g)
- 2 tsp canna butter (10 g)
- 3 tbsp soy sauce (40 ml)
- Pinch of pepper

**Cook:**
Cut the asparagus diagonally into 1/4-inch (10 mm) slices.
In a large frying pan, sauté asparagus until tender in the 2 mixed butters, for about 6 minutes.
But 2 minutes before the end of cooking, add the soy sauce and pepper.
Serves 4 to 6.

# Cannabis Artichoke Dip

**Ingredients:**
- 1 1/2 cups raw cashew nuts (110 g)
- 1 1/2 cups unsweetened plain almond milk (375 ml)
- 4 tbsp freshly squeezed lemon juice (60 ml)
- 4 medium to large garlic cloves
- 2 tsp nutritional yeast (10 g)
- 1 1/2 teaspoon sea salt (7 g)
- 1 tsp dry mustard (5 g)
- 10 tsp cannabis-infused coconut oil (50 ml)

- 2 cans of artichoke hearts, drained and chopped
- 4 cups Swiss card beets or spinach

**Cook:**

Preheat the oven to 375 degrees F (190 C)

Combine all ingredients and mix first and then let it soak for 1 1/2 hours in the blender.

Then empty the contents of the blender into a large bowl.

Stir in 2 cans of artichoke hearts, drained and chopped, 4 cups shredded Swiss beetroot (can be replaced with spinach)

Mix and pour into an oven-proof dish (12 x10) and bake for 25–30 minutes or until the cannabis artichoke dip is golden and warm in the center.

Allow to cool for 15 to 20 minutes before serving.

10 to 12 servings.

# Italian Canna Pizza pause

**Ingredients:**
- 1/3 cup Parmesan or Romano cheese (75 g)
- 4 slices of white bread or whole wheat, cut into small pieces.
- 1 lb, fresh or frozen spinach, chopped (454 g)
- 1 cup chopped parsley (210 g)
- 1 medium onion, chopped
- 1/3 cup softened butter (75 g)
- 2 tsp canna butter (10 g)
- 1/4 teaspoon basil (1 g)
- 1/4 tsp oregano (1 g)
- 1 tsp salt (5 g)
- A pinch of pepper
- 3 eggs, beaten
- 1 clove minced garlic

**Cook:**

In a large bowl, combine all ingredients and mix.

Dispose the bread into an 8-inch (20.32 cm) greased square dishes.

Pour the mixed ingredients equally on the bread.

Bake at 325 degrees F (160 C) for 30 or 40 minutes, or until the top is golden brown.

Cut into squares as it would be a pizza.

Serve 4 to 6 servings.

**READ THIS: (in addition)**

This cannabis cookbook can become a simple cookbook, without cannabis; just remove the cannabis ingredient in the recipe. You can do the same with your own favorite recipes. But, there are basic to follow, by transforming your recipes.

# CHAPTER 7

# MARINADE, spreadable butters

**Warning:**
Since it is impossible for us to know what intensities and qualities of cannabis you have on hand, it is also impossible for us to speculate on the dosage of your food. So, the quantities applied to each recipe, are only a suggestion, speculating that you use products of good quality and adequate intensity. So, as a matter of wisdom, be careful in your dosages and start by experimenting with small dosages of cannabis at once and progress little by little. But don't take the risk of cooking and ingesting garbage products from the black market. Unless insecticides and dubious mixtures make your trip... If you think it's OK for you, then smoke them, but at least don't destroy your stomach and your immune system ingesting that junk... Love life!

**Marinades:**
Marinades and spread butters are induced with canna butter, so simply marinate your meats, beef, pork, chicken or wild meats.
And for the butters to spread, treat yourself on crackers or on your morning toast...

# MARINADE IN THE BEER Canna

## For chicken and pork

Ingredients:
- 12 oz beer or apple juice (340 ml)
- 1 cup chopped onions (210 g)
- 1/4 cup lemon juice (50 ml)
- 2 tbsp instant chicken broth (30 ml)
- 3 tbsp vegetable oil (45 ml)
- 2 teaspoons of your canna oil (10 ml)
- 2 to 3 garlic cloves, chopped

**Cook:**
Mix all ingredients in a medium bowl and use it to marinate chicken, beef or pork chops.

Marinate in the refrigerator for 4 hours or overnight.

Turn over once in a while.

Cook the meat on the grill to the desired degree and brush the meat, with the rest of the marinade.

Make about 2 cups of marinade (500 ml).

You can make the same recipe with a leftover red or white wine.

# GREK Canna MARINADE

## Lemon and basil

Ingredients:
- 3 garlic cloves, chopped
- 1 tbsp salt (15 g)
- 1 cup olive or vegetable oil (250 ml)
- 2 teaspoons of your canna oil (10 ml)
- The grated peel and juice of 4 lemons

- **1 tbsp basil (15 g)**

**Cook:**
In a large bowl, crush garlic and salt.
Pour in the rest of the ingredients.
Marinate meat for 4 hours or overnight.
This marinade is delicious on any kind of meat, but especially on chicken, lamb, on skewers.
Makes 1 1/2 to 2 cups marinades. (350 ml to 500 ml)

# LIVER PÂTÉ VIKING Canna

**Ingredients:**
- **1 lb of liver pâté (450 g)**
- **2 tsp canna butter (10 g)**
- **1/2 cup softened butter or margarine (125 g)**
- **1/4-cup Irish Mist (60 ml)**
- **2 tbsp grated shallots (25 g)**
- **3 1/4 oz pitted and sliced black olives (110 g)**
- **Fresh ground pepper.**

**Cook:**
Mix well together the liver pâté and butters.
Add ingredients and mix again.
Place in a small baking dish pan and refrigerate.
Delicious to spread on slices of crusty toasted bread or crackers.
The paste can also be unmolded off and garnished with red pepper edges and tufts of parsley for degustation.

# CRESSON Cana BUTTER

**Ingredients:**
- 1 cup softened butter (250 g)
- 2 tsp canna butter (10 g)
- 1 tsp paprika (5 g)
- 1/2 cup finely chopped watercress (110 g)

**Cook:**

Mix all the ingredients. (If desired, use a mixer or robot.)

Place it in the refrigerator.

Substitute mayonnaise for sandwiches or use it as an appetizer on crackers or roasted bread.

# Eggplant pizza Canna

**Ingredients:**
- 1 medium eggplant
- 1/2 cup melted butter (125 ml)
- 2 teaspoons of your canna oil (10 g)
- 3/4 cup fine breadcrumbs (175 g)
- 1/4 tsp salt (1 g)
- 1 cup spaghetti tomato sauce (250 ml)
- 1 tbsp oregano (15 g)
- 1 cup grated cheese (250 g)

**Cook:**

Remove the peel from the eggplant and cut into 1/2 inch (127 cm) slices.

Dip the slices in mixed butter and canna oil, then in breadcrumbs, mixed with salt.

Place on greased baking sheet.

Place sauce on top of each slice.

Sprinkle with oregano and cheese. (The slices will look like miniature pizza.)

Bake at 450 degrees (225 C) for 10 to 12 minutes, or until golden.

Makes 4 servings.

# HERBS & Cauliflower Canna

Ingredients:
- 1 full cauliflower
- 2 tbsp butter (30 ml)
- 2 tsp canna butter (10 g)
- 1 tbsp fresh chopped parsley (15 ml)
- 1 tbsp chopped chives (15 ml)
- Salt and pepper to taste
- A pinch of cayenne pepper or Tabasco sauce

Cook:

Wash the cauliflower and remove the green leaves.

Cut to the heart, keep the head intact.

In a large pot, bring one inch of water (3 cm) to a boil.

Place cauliflower in the cooking pot, cauliflower tail in the bottom and steam, cover for 15 to 20 minutes, or until the cauliflower is tender.

Place on a hot serving dish.

Mix herbs and seasonings with melted butter and canna butter, and spread over cauliflower.

Makes 4 to 6 servings.

# LIVER PÂTÉ Canna

Ingredients:
- 2 lbs chicken liver (1 kg)
- 3 sprigs of parsley

- **1 bay leaf**
- **Thyme**
- **1 cup melted butter (250 ml)**
- **Salt**
- **2 tsp canna butter (10 g)**
- **1 1/2 teaspoons prepared mustard (7 g)**
- **1/4 tsp nail (1.5 g)**
- **Cayenne**
- **Nutmeg**
- **Cognac to taste**

**Cook:**

Place the livers in a saucepan; cover with water and add parsley, bay leaf and thyme.

Cover and simmer for 20 minutes.

Drain, cut and pass with a meat processor.

Mix the liver with the butter and canna butter, salt, mustard, nail, cayenne and nutmeg.

Add the Cognac. Beat vigorously.

Place in a pan and cool.

Serve on croutons or crackers.

You ca try something else with a mix of gizzards, liver and hearts.

# CHAPTER 8

# FULL meals

Since it is impossible for us to know what intensities and qualities of cannabis you have in hand, it is also impossible for us to speculate on the dosage of your food. But, the quantities applied to each recipe, are only a suggestion, speculating that you use products of good quality and adequate intensity. So, as a matter of wisdom, be careful in your dosages and start by experimenting with small dosages of cannabis at once and progress little by little.

## Consumption TRUCS:

Remember that the main trick for the pleasure of floating, to last a long time, is to eat lightly and never ingest cannabis when your stomach is full; or 50% of the expected effects will quickly go into your 30 feet of the bowel, and that, along with your investment.

Also, not too sweet and not too fat; however, it appears that a little sweetness and a little fat, hang on the effect. And alcohol even more, because alcohol goes directly into the bloodstream through the stomach membranes; instead of going through the digestive system or by the lungs for smokers.

# BEEF CUBES IN THE MEXI-canna
## (One of the best reviews)

Ingredients:
- 2 lbs of beef cut in cubes (1 kg)
- 2 tsp olive oil (10 ml)
- 2 tsp canna butter (10 g)
- 1 cup onions (250 ml)
- 1 green chili
- 1/2 cup celery (125 ml)
- 1 cup mushrooms (250 ml)
- 2 tsp cornstarch (10 g)
- 1 1/2 cups canned tomatoes (375 ml)
- 1 tsp salt (5 g)
- 1 tsp pepper 95 g)
- 4 to 6 potatoes

Cook:

Lightly sear the meat placed in the bottom of a pot, stirring in very little cooking oil. This action will help the meat to stay tender (but never and only add salt to the sauce, so as not to harden the meat.)

Cover meat with all vegetables cut into pieces, onions, chili, celery and mushrooms.

Then in another pot, for the sauce:

Heat the tomatoes and simmer until boiling.

In a mixing pot, combine the cornstarch with a little cold water and mix well with your canna butter and the rest of the oil, and after you gradually add the cornstarch to thicken the tomato sauce.

Pour the sauce over beef and vegetables, add the seasoning and the potatoes in pieces.

Bake for an hour and a half at 350 degrees F (180 C)

# TURKEY with CURRY Canna

Ingredients:
- 1/4 cup butter (57 g)
- 2 tsp canna butter
- 1/4 cup flour (57 g)
- 1/2 to 1 tsp curry powder (3 g to 5 g)
- 3 ml to 5 ml 1/4 teaspoon salt (1 ml)
- Pepper suspicion
- 2 cups milk (500 ml)

Here is the rest of the ingredients
- 2 cups cooked turkey, cut (454 g)
- 1 can of 20 oz (567 g) drained pineapple pieces
- 1 1/2 cups chopped celery (341 g)
- 1/2 cup sliced almonds or dry-roasted peanuts (114 g)

Cook:
In a medium pot, melt butter mixed with canna butter.
Stir, adding flour, curry powder, salt, and pepper.
Gradually stir in the milk.
Cook over medium heat, stirring constantly until thickened and stir in remaining ingredients. Serve over hot rice, noodles, cookies or toast.

## SIMPLE STUFFING
Without or with Canna.

Ingredients:
- 1 lb minced meat (of your choice) (454 g)
- 2 cups fresh breadcrumbs
- 1 cup celery (250 ml)
- 1 chopped onion

- **3 tbsp melted butter (40 g)**
- **2 tsp canna butter (optionnels)**
- **1/2 tbsp salt (7 g)**
- **1/2 tsp pepper (2 g)**

**Cook:**
**Seasonings according to the meat used:**

**Beef:** thyme, marjoram, savory, celery powder, parsley, Dijon, garlic.

**Veal:** thyme, chives, parsley, tarragon, bay leaf, savory, garlic, celery powder.

**Pork:** garlic, sage, ground cloves, Marjolaine Bay leaves, parsley, savory, paprika.
Brown the ground meat.
Add remaining ingredients and mix well.
If any one of the meat does not include canna butter, then you can include 2 tsp canna butter in the stuffing.

# SWEET Potatoes Canna

**Ingredients:**
- **4 lbs of sweet potatoes (1.81 kg)**
- **3/4 cup butter (170 g)**
- **2 teaspoons of your canna oil (10 ml)**
- **1/2 cup honey or maple syrup (125 ml)**
- **3 tbsp water (40 ml)**
- **1 tbsp ground allspice (15 ml)**
- **1 cup coarsely chopped walnuts (227 g)**

**Cook:**

Peel the potatoes and cook in boiling water covered until almost tender.

Cool and slice into 1/4-inch thick (O.16 cm) slices.

Set aside.

In a medium pot, combine butter, canna oil, honey, water and allspice.

Mix 2 tablespoons (30 ml) of butter mixture with the nuts and set aside.

Place half of the sweet potatoes in a 13 x 9-inch (33 x 23 cm) baking dish.

Spoon over 1/3 of the butter mixture over the potatoes.

Cover with remaining potatoes.

Return the rest of the butter mixture to the top. Cook uncovered at 400 degrees F (200 C) for 30 minutes or until hot.

Sprinkle with walnuts. Cook for another 5 minutes.

Serves 10

# Squash & Orange Canna

**Ingredients:**
- 3 cups cooked squash, crushed (680 g)
- 1/2 cup butter (125 ml)
- 2 teaspoons of your canna oil
- 1/2 cup brown sugar or honey (114 g)
- The juice and zest of an orange
- 1 tsp salt (5 ml)
- 1/8 tsp pepper (O.5 ml)

**COOK:**
Combine all ingredients and mix well. Cook over a slow heat and stir constantly, until hot, about 5 minutes.

Then, pour into a pint (0.57 liters) saucepan and cook uncovered at 350 degrees F (180 C) for about 30 minutes or until cooked through.

Makes 4 to 6 servings.

# RICE and Spinach Canna

Ingredients:
- 1/2 cup softened butter (125 ml)
- 2 teaspoons of your canna oil (10 ml)
- 1/2 cup chopped onions (125 ml)
- 1 1/2 cups grated Cheddar cheese (375 ml)
- 2 eggs, beaten
- 2 cups milk (500 ml)
- 1 cup uncooked rice (250 ml)
- 1 lb cooked and chopped spinach
- (454 g) or 1 packet of frozen spinach
- 1 tsp garlic salt (5 ml)

Mix all the ingredients and pour into a 2-pint saucepan (about 2 liters).

Cover and cook at 350 degrees (180 C) for 40 minutes and remove the lid and cook for another 20 minutes.

Makes 10 servings.

# Spaghetti and Broccoli Canna

Ingredients:
- 1 lb of spaghetti (454 g) cooked and drained
- 2 lbs fresh broccoli (900 g)
- 2 10 oz packets (300 ml) broccoli, cut, frozen.
- 3/4 tsp salt (4 ml)

- 1 1/2 cups water (375 ml)
- 1/4 cup olive oil or melted butter (50 ml)
- 2 tsp canna butter
- 1/4 teaspoon pepper (1 ml)
- Shredded Parmesan cheese.

**Cook:**
If using fresh broccoli, cut into 2-inch (5 cm) pieces.
Cook fresh or frozen broccoli in salted water until tender.
Sauté pasta and broccoli with a small amount of mixed cooking water, mixed oil and canna butter, pepper and 1/2 cup (125 ml) Parmesan cheese.
Serve immediately, on the hot mat of spaghetti, sprinkle with more Parmesan cheese if desired.
Makes 4 to 6 servings.

# Italian pasta with cheese & garlic
USE the pasta of your choice with Canna or not.

**Ingredients:**
- 2 or 3 tablespoons canna butter (30–45 g)
- Pasta of your choice, spaghetti (ideal)
- Salt and pepper
- 1 teaspoon olive oil (5 g)
- Seven garlic cloves, chopped
- 1 cup Parmesan cheese (240 g)

**Cook:**
Melt olive oil and your canna butter in a large skillet over medium heat.
Add the garlic to the butter and cook until lightly browned and remove from the heat and set aside.
Boil your pasta in a large pot and add a little salt to the water.

Cook until tender (about 10 minutes), then drain the water from the pasta.

Keep, about 1/4 cup from the pasta-cooking-water.

Then:

Then put the pasta back in the pan with 1/4 cup of the pasta water, and add to the mixture of canna butters infused with garlic and mixed with olive oil, and then salt and pepper to your liking.

Mix all the ingredients well with your pasta, so that your canna-butter mixture adheres to the pasta, then spread over the Parmesan cheese.

6 - 8 PORTIONS

# RICE AND BROCCOLI Canna

**Ingredients:**
- **2 cups hot water (500 ml)**
- **1 1/2 oz (28.3 g) packet of onion soup mix**
- **1 cup uncooked rice (240 g)**
- **2 tbsp butter (25 g)**
- **2 tsp of your canna oil (10 ml)**
- **1/2 tsp salt (2 g)**
- **1/4 tsp pepper (1 g)**
- **1 packet of 10 on frozen and cut broccoli (300 g)**

**Cook:**
In a 2-pint (2.26L) pot with a tight lid, combine hot water and the soup packet mix, rice, butter, canna oil, salt and pepper.

Stir very well.

Place frozen broccoli in the middle.

Cover and cook at 375 degrees F (190 C) for 45 minutes or until rice is cooked and liquid is absorbed.

Move gently with a fork before serving.

Serves 4 people.

# RATATOUILLE Canna

**Ingredients:**
- 2 medium onions, peeled and chopped
- 1 clove garlic, chopped
- 5 tbsp olive oil (75 ml)
- 3 tsp canna butter (15 g)
- 2 medium zucchini sliced
- 2 small eggplants, peeled and cubed
- 2 medium green peppers, sliced
- 5 medium tomatoes, quartered
- 1 tsp basil (5 g)
- 2 tbsp chopped parsley (25 g)
- 1 tsp salt (5 g)
- 1/4 tsp pepper (1 g)
- Parmesan cheese

**Cook:**

In a large frying pan, sauté onions and garlic in oil for 5 minutes.

Add zucchini, eggplant and green peppers.

Stir gently and sauté for another 10 minutes.

Add tomatoes, the canna butter and remaining ingredients.

Reduce heat, cover and simmer for 10 to 15 minutes.

If desired, sprinkle with Parmesan cheese.

Serve hot or cold.

Makes 6 servings.

# Fish

Since we cannot know what intensity and quality of cannabis you have in hand, and that it would also be impossible for us to speculate on the dosage of your food? But, the quantities applied to each recipe, are only a suggestion, speculating that you use products of good quality and adequate intensity. So, as a matter of wisdom, be careful in your dosages and start by experimenting with small dosages of cannabis at once and progress little by little.

## FISH fillet Canna

**Ingredients:**
- **2 lbs of fish (cod fillet, sole or halibut steaks (1 kg).**
- **1/2 tsp salt (2 ml)**
- **1/2 tsp paprika (2 ml)**
- **A little Cayenne**
- **Juice of 1 lemon**
- **1/2 cup or more, sliced onions (125 ml)**
- **1 tbsp butter (15 g)**
- **2 tsp canna butter (mixed with butter) (10 g)**
- **Green pepper rings**

**Cook:**
Place fillets in a greased, shallow dish.
Combine salt, pepper, paprika, cayenne and lemon juice.
Pour over the fish.
Soften the onions and peppers in the melted butters, then arrange over the fish, alternating the onion and chili slices and pour in the remaining butter.

Preheat the oven at 235 F (170 C) and bake for 15 minutes or until ready.

For more flavor, but not included in the original recipe.

If desired, stuff the fish and bake. But if you stuff the fish, use the canna butter only in the stuff, because using it in both the recipes would maybe too high in intensity...

# FARCE FOR POISSON-canna

**Ingredients:**
- **2 cups bread (500 ml)**
- **1 chopped onion**
- **1 egg yolk**
- **1 tsp butter (5 ml)**
- **2 tsp canna butter (mixed with butter) (10 g)**
- **Salt, pepper**
- **Savory**
- **A little cold water**

**Cook:**

Soften the bread in cold water.

Drain and knead.

Add a lightly fried onion to the butter, salt, pepper, savory and egg yolk.

Stuff the fish.

Make about 1 1/2 cups (341 g)

**READ THIS:** (in addition)

This cannabis cookbook can become a simple cookbook, without cannabis; just remove the cannabis ingredient in the recipe. You can do the same with your own favorite recipes. But, there are basic to follow, by transforming your recipes.

# Reflection Sector

## Endocannabinoid system

The endocannabinoid system is a system of cannabinoid receptors throughout our body and connected to the brains of almost all humans and animals. The receptors in the endocannabinoid system of each living being are individual as a fingerprint, which would be why each of us would react differently to each product of diverse strains.

So know your strain, which may be relational to your cannabinoid receptors.

Whether it is a psychological problem such as insomnia or anxiety or a physical problem such as pain, inflammation or diabetes, cannabis can probably provide safe, effective and 100% natural relief.

Simply said, it is just our body's natural marijuana system: able to influence a range of "mind and body" functions to promote health and homeostasis to probably every circuit of our body.

**Do some research on the net:**

(Research extracted from Dr. Dustin Sulak from: The National Organization for the Reform of Cannabis Laws).

Homeotasis: Stabilization of different physiological constants in living organisms.

**The more you know, the less you believe!**

Publisher : www.jasselin.com

# CHAPTER 9

# RAGING 4 foods after smoking?

Cannabis opens the appetite, but do not eat more canna things if you are in a "high".

## Burrito pizza (without canna)

You just want to calm your cravings, so don't use other cannabis dishes.

Ingredients:
- Roll buns, number according to your guests
- Marinara sauce
- Cheese (lots)
- Banana puree
- Pepperoni.

Cook:

Preheat the oven to 350 F (180 C).

Prepare the amount of your ingredients according to the number of your guests in cravings and mash one or two bananas.

Cut the buns in half

Remove some of the crumbs from the bread and eat it with a little butter while waiting for your pizza burrito.

Stuff your breads generously with the banana paste, pepperoni and cheese spread inside.

Slowly fill your burrito with marinara sauce.

Cover the top with more cheese.

Bake at 350 degrees (180 C) for 8–10 minutes.

Watch the oven so you don't burn your treats.

# Peanut butter and banana sandwich (no canna)

**Spread:**
Toast the bread.

Cut the banana into thin slices.

Spread the peanut butter over the bread.

Put as many banana slices as you like.

Sprinkle with cinnamon sugar (optional).

Put the two pieces of bread together. (Do not wait, rrrrr.)

# ICE CREAM served with cereal but (no canna)

An ice cream to your liking and the cereal you have in hand, it's quick and your gullet will be soothed.

**Here you go:**
Pour your cereal into a dish, with just a little soy milk or almond in the bottom and cover with ice cream and enjoy.

**But, the most popular snacks are pizzas, it's so easy, you take your cell phone and order it.**

# CHAPTER 10

# DESSERTS

## Beware of desserts:

Watch out for desserts, they're sneaky, they're good, they call you and don't get out of your head. The danger is to intoxicate yourself without realizing it, not eating too much, one after the other. Watch the children, especially, don't take the risk of leaving them within their reach, your good little brownies. One, OK, wait for the effect and two, maybe if you know the dosage!

## SESAME buttered Balls Canna

Ingredients:
- 1 cup softened butter (227 g)
- 1 tsp canna butter (5 g) mixed with butter
- 1/4 cup sugar (57 g)
- 1 tsp almond extract (5 ml)
- 1/2 tsp salt (3 ml)
- 2 cups flour (454 g)
- Sesame seeds
- Jam (raspberries, strawberries, apricots or peaches)

Cook:
Bring butter, canna butter and sugar in some kind of cream.

Mix the almond extract and salt in it.

Add flour and mix well.

Form tablespoons of pasta into the shape of balls and roll them into the sesame seeds.

Place on parchment paper on a baking sheet.

Squeeze your finger into the center of each biscuit and fill with jam.

Bake at 400 F (200 C) for 10 to 12 minutes, or until it starts to brown.

Make about three dozen.

# PECAN'S Sweeties Canna

**Ingredients:**
- 3 cups firmly pressed brown sugar (680 g)
- 1 cup thick cream (250 ml)
- 1/4 cup butter (57 g)
- 3 tsp canna butter (10 g to 15 g)
- 2 tbsp corn syrup
- 1/4 teaspoon salt (1 ml)
- 1 tsp vanilla (5 ml)
- 2 cups large pieces of pecans (454 g)

**Cook:**
In a pot of 3/4 pints (1L 1/2), combine sugar, cream, butter, corn syrup and salt.

Bring to a boil over medium heat, stirring to dissolve sugar.

Continue cooking, stirring constantly, until the candy thermometer marks 236 degrees F (112 C) (soft ball state).

Remove from heat and leave aside for 5 minutes.

Stir the vanilla and walnuts in it.

Beat with a wooden spoon until the mixture thickens and loses its shine.

Drop by teaspoon on waxed paper to form small patties around 2 inches in diameter.

Let it cool.

Wrap individually in wax or plastic paper.

Store in a cool and dry place.

Make around three dozen.

# CANna oatmeal GALETTES

**Ingredients:**

- 3 cups shaved fast-cooked oatmeal (680 g)
- 2/3 cup sugar (78 g)
- 1/2 cup flour (114 g)
- 1/2 tsp salt (3 ml)
- 3/4 cup softened butter (170 g)
- 2 tsp of your coconut-canna oil or canna butter
- 1 tsp vanilla (5 ml)

**COOK:**

In a large bowl, combine oatmeal, sugar, flour and salt.

Add the butter, the coco canna oil, vanilla and mix well until the mixture becomes uniform.

Dispose the blend of a well greased baking sheet.

Bake at 350 degrees F (180 C) for 25 to 30 minutes, or until brown.

Let it cool a little and while still warm, cut into equal scare cookies.

Cool and place on parchment paper.

Make about 3 dozen cookies.

# Carrot cake with canna oil

## Ingredients:
- 3/4 cup clear sugar (175 g)
- 1 cup sunflower oil (175 ml)
- 1/8 cup canna oil (40 ml) (adjust intensity if necessary)
- 3 large eggs, lightly beaten
- 5 oz grated carrots (140 g)
- 3 1/2 oz raisins (100 g)
- The grated zest of a large orange
- 2/3 cup self-lifting flour (175 g)
- 1 teaspoon baking soda (5 ml)
- 1 teaspoon cinnamon powder (5 ml)
- 1/2 teaspoon grated nutmeg (freshly grated will give you the best flavor) (3 ml)

## Cook:
Preheat the oven to 350 F (180 C).

Oil the bottom and sides of a cake pan and dispose of parchment paper in it.

In a large bowl, mix the sugar, the oil, the canna oil and the eggs and stir into grated carrots, raisins and orange zest.

Then mix the flour, baking soda and spices and smooth well in the bowl and the mixture into the cake pan and bake for 45 minutes.

When baking close to 35–40 minutes, check with the toothpick trick, to see if it's still sticky inside, if so, let it cook for another 5–7 minutes.

Allow to cool a little in the pan and turn it over on a wax paper, remove the first bottom paper and let it cool.

Cut into small pieces and coat with icing sugar.

# THE BROWNIES

**DOSAGES, caution:**
Since it is impossible for us to know what intensities and qualities of cannabis you have in hand, it is also impossible for us to speculate on the dosage of your food. However, the quantities applied to each recipe are only a suggestion, speculating that you use products of good quality and adequate intensity. So, as a matter of wisdom, be careful in your dosages and start by experimenting with small dosages of cannabis at once and progress little by little.

## Light Brownies Canna

Brownies, blonds are light, that's what you need in your digestive system; don't forget that an overcharged stomach reacts badly and your High could be evaporated into the large intestine quickly and that's not what you want.

**Ingredients:**
- 1 ounce canna butter (about 2 tablespoons) (30 g)
- 6 tablespoons butter (90 g)
- 1 cup dark brown sugar (200 g)
- 1 large egg or two small eggs
- 1 1/2 teaspoons vanilla extract (8 ml)
- 1 pinch of sea salt (1 g)
- 1 1/8 cup all-purpose flour or whole wheat (140 g)

The following ingredients, all or according to your choice:
- 1/2 cup chocolate chips (38 g)
- 1/4 cup of favorite liqueur (65 ml)
- 1/2 cup toasted walnuts (38 g)
- 1/2 cup dried fruit or shredded coconut (38 g)
- 1/2 teaspoon of a flavoring extract, depending on taste (3 ml)

**Cook:**

Preheat your oven to 350 degrees Fahrenheit (180 C).

Prepare a medium-sized, greased cake dish or insert parchment paper.

Then mix the cannabis butter, salted butter and brown sugar in a large bowl until well blended.

Then add the egg, vanilla extract and mix again.

Finally, add the flour and one of the extra ingredients you might wish for.

Beat it all, up to becoming dough, with a whisk or electric mixer, until the mixture is thick and homogeneous.

Pour the mixed dough into the baking dish and place it in the oven and cook for 22–25 minutes or until the top is crunchy and firm.

(As we always do, insert a toothpick to check if your brownies are cooked properly.)

Allow them to cool for 30 minutes to 1 hour, depending on your preferences. Cut in egal pieces and enjoy but eat reasonably.

Your favorite essences: chocolate, almond, strawberry, raspberry, mint, rum (or coconut if your Cana fat is coconut).

Sers : about 20 pieces.

# Brownie coco-canna

A reinvented delight that no one can ignore. It's too easy to eat too much, don't fall for it...

**ingredient:**

- 12 ounces sweet and sour chocolate (375 ml)
- 3 sticks of salted butter (375 g)
- 3 tablespoons canna butter (45 g)
- 1 3/4 cups brown sugar (350 g)

- 1 tablespoon vanilla extract (15 ml)
- 6 medium eggs
- 1 1/2 cups whole wheat flour or all-purpose flour (188 g)
- 1 teaspoon sea salt (5 g)
- 1/8 cup cocoa powder, unsweetened (30 g)
- 1/2 cup favorite chocolate chips (55 g)
- 1/2 cup macadamia nuts (45 g) (Queensland nut)

## Cook:

Start by preheating the oven to 350 F. (180 C)

In a medium saucepan over low heat, melt together sweet and sour chocolate, canna oil and salted butter, stirring continuously until very liquid (watch out for not burning, but salted butter performs better in heat).

Remove from heat and let it cool for a few minutes.

## Then:

In another large bowl, combine brown sugar, vanilla extract and eggs, beating and mixing well until smooth.

As soon as your chocolate mixture and butters have cooled a little, transfer the mixture slowly into your large bowl, stirring it with eggs, sugar and vanilla extract, whisking always until a homogeneous consistency.

## Finally:

Stir in salt, cocoa powder, flour, and the chocolate chips, and still stirring until smooth.

Prepare a baking pan and cover it with parchment paper or a silicone mold.

Spread your brownie mixture in your pan and bake for about 25 minutes, or until dry toothpick shows that your brownies are cooked through.

Cut the brownies into 20 pieces and cool.

You will enjoy as long as about 20 pieces.

# Brownies Canna Vanilla

Your reputation as a host will not be diminished with these delicious brownies, especially when your guest is returning home after a night partying with you...

Ingredients:
- 2 large medium or large eggs
- 1 teaspoon vanilla extract (5 ml)
- 1/4 teaspoon sea salt (2 g)
- 1/4 teaspoon baking powder (2 g)
- 1 cup brown sugar (200 g)
- 1/2 cup whole or all-purpose wheat flour (70 g)
- 1/3 cup cocoa powder (38 g)
- 1/4 cup coconut-canna oil (60 g)
- 1/4 cup sunflower oil or light vegetable oil (65 ml)
- 4 Graham cookies
- 8 ounces milk chocolate, powdered (240 g)
- 1 cup mini marshmallows (115 g)

Cook:
Preheat the oven to 350 F (180 C).

You need a medium and deep oven cake plate, well oiled or sulfurised paper or if you have special silicone baking plates.

And then, in a large bowl mix together eggs, vanilla extract, sea salt, baking powder and brown sugar.

Once well mixed, add wheat flour, cocoa powder, coconut-canna oil and sunflower oil.

Pour this mixture into the baking dish and place in the oven for 15 minutes.

While the brownie mixture is cooking, in another bowl, mix the crushed Graham cookies, milk chocolate and marshmallows.

After the brownies have cooked for about 15 minutes, remove from the oven and sprinkle with the mixture of Graham's cookies, milk chocolate and marshmallow pieces.

Bake for another 15 to 18 minutes or until a toothpick comes out dry. (As we used to do!)

Let the brownies cool a little and cut them into 12 super delicious pieces.

Serves: about 12 pieces.

# Veggie-canna brownies

In reality, all recipes can be converted to the vegan. It is specially invented for those who choose that their health is above all; but, without sacrificing the pleasure of tasting reasonably.

**Ingredients:**
- 3/4 cup dairy-free dark chocolate (85 g)
- 1/2 cup self-lifting flour (60 g)
- 4 tablespoons unsweetened cocoa powder (32 g)
- 1/8 teaspoon sea salt (1 g)
- 1/2 cup caster sugar (80 g)
- 1 teaspoon vanilla extract (5 g)
- 2 tablespoons coconut butter or cannabis coconut oil (30 g)
- Cup of unsweetened soy milk, almond or coconut (to taste)
- 3 tablespoons sunflower oil (45 ml)
- 1/2 cup chopped pecans (40 g)

**Cook:**
Preheat your oven to 350 F (180 C)

Prepare for later, a baking sheet in the oven, covered with sulfirised paper or a silicone plate.

Using a set of double boilers or a large cooking pot with a few inches of hot water, place into it a smaller cooking pot in which you will melt, so as not to stick, your dark chocolate without dairy products.

Immediately melted, set aside, out of the double boiler.

In a large separate bowl, combine self-raising flour and unsweetened cocoa powder, then add sea salt and powdered sugar.

Then mix and add vanilla extract, vegetable coconut butter with cannabis, soy milk and melted chocolate, just done.

Mix until the mixture is even and not too dense.

Add the chopped pecans and sunflower oil (optional).

Pour the mixture into your baking sheet and bake for 22–25 minutes.

At around 22 minutes, let's do the usual toothpick test.

Take out the brownies and let them cool for about 10 minutes.

Cut into 18 pieces.

Sers : about 18 pieces.

# Canna Muffins Adapted

**For people who are gluten intolerant or have celiac disease will have the pleasure of feasting too on this little cannabis treat.**

**Ingredients:**
- 1 cup almond flour, or any ones you pick. (115 g)
- 1/8 teaspoon sea salt (1 g)
- 1/4 teaspoon baking soda (1 g)
- 1/2 cup cocoa powder (55 g)
- 1 teaspoon vanilla extract (5 ml)
- 3 large eggs
- 1/4 cup melted coconut oil (65 ml)
- 1/4 cup canna butter and—or coconut canna (60 g)
- 1/2 cup honey (165 g)

**Cook:**
Start by preheating your oven to 350 F (180 C).
In a large bowl, combine almond flour, sea salt, baking soda, cocoa powder and vanilla extract.
In another smaller bowl, mix together the eggs, the coconut oil and canna butter. (Or the canna coco oil)
Add this mixture to the first larger bowl of the dry ingredients.
Mix everything together and mix in the honey until homogeneous.
Grease your pan with coconut fat and pour the mixture into the mini muffin tray,
place the tray in the oven for 16 to 19 minutes.
Once cooked well, they will be easily removed from the tray.
If they seem to stick, pass the toot pick test and they may have to cook for a little more.
Let it cool a little and garnish the way you like.

# MUFFINS AU SON Canna (pasta)
A recipe for muffin cooking dough (keep refrigerated)

**Ingredients:**
- 2 cups 100% bran (454 g) (cereal)
- 2 cups boiling water (500 ml)
- 1 cup melted butter (250 ml)
- 2 tsp canna butter
- 2 cups sugar (454 g)
- 4 eggs
- 1 pint of butter milk or plain yogurt (1000 ml)
- 5 cups flour (1135 g)
- 5 tsp baking soda (25 ml)
- 1 tsp salt (5 ml)
- 4 cups of bran cereal (flakes, germs, filaments [909 g]

- **1 cup grapes [227 g]**

**Cook:**

In a large bowl, pour boiling water over the sound and let stand.

In a large mixing bowl, put the butter and sugar in cream. Add eggs and beat well.

Stir in butter milk and mix of sound and water.

Combine flour, baking soda, salt and cereals.

Add to moist mixture, stirring until blended. [Do not use the electric mixer.]

Put the grapes in.

Fill 2/3 of the muffin pans and bake at 400 degrees F [200 C] for 25 minutes.

The dough can be kept in the refrigerator in a closed container for 6 to 8 weeks.

Do not stir before use; only take the desired amount.

Makes about 1 1/2 gallons of dough [5.68 liters].

# BANANA Spread

**For cake or toast**

**Ingredients:**
- **1/4 cup softened butter [50 ml]**
- **1/2 cup cocoa Fry [125 ml]**
- **1/4 cup mashed bananas [50 ml]**
- **2 tbsp milk [25 ml]**
- **1/2 tsp vanilla [2 ml]**
- **3 cups icing sugar [700 ml]**

Mix well evenly and apply generously on any of your favorite cakes or tarts. Well made, this finely treat will last in the refrigerator for a long time.

# Cream of sugar Canna

Ingredients:
- **5 tbsp melted butter [50 ml]**
- **2 tsp canna butter or coconut-canna oil**
- **2 cups brown sugar [500 ml]**
- **1/2 cup cream 35% [125 ml] or,**
- **1/2 cup Carnation milk.**

Mix well and boil for exactly 5 minutes.
Remove from heat.
Add 2 cups [500 ml] brown sugar and 1 teaspoon [5 ml] vanilla.
Mix everything and pour into a mold.

# Pancakes Canna

Ingredients:
- **1/4 cup flour [22 S ml]**
- **2 tbsp sugar [25 ml]**
- **Salt**
- **3 eggs**
- **1 cup milk [250 ml]**
- **2 tbsp butter [25 ml]**
- **1 tsp canna butter**

Mix it all up. Cook in an oil-induced frying pan.
Makes about 6 pancakes.

# MOTHER's Doughnut
## For the holidays [no canna]

Ingredients:
- 3 tbsp butter [40 ml]
- 1 cup sugar [250 ml]
- 2 eggs
- 1 tsp baking soda [5 ml]
- 1 cup milk [250 ml]
- 2 cups flour [500 ml]
- 2 tsp cream of tartar [l0 ml]
- 1/2 tsp nutmeg [2 ml]
- 1 tsp vanilla essence [5 ml]

Cook:
Break the butter into cream and add sugar and eggs.
Dissolve the bicarbonate in the milk and add to the mixture.
Sift the flour and cream of tartar and add it to the mixture with the nutmeg and vanilla essence.
After mixing everything together, let the dough cool overnight.
The next day, roll it thin and prune round dough with a glass.
Dip the glass in flour for not to stick up with the dough mix.
Cook in the boiling grease pot or hot oil.

# HUM! COOKIES and Canna

Ingredients:
- 3/4 cup butter [225 ml]
- 2 tsp canna butter [mixed with butter]
- 1/3 cup brown sugar [75 ml]
- 2 egg yolks

- 1 1/2 cups sifted flour [350 ml]
- 2 egg whites
- 1 1/4 cups chopped walnuts [200 ml]
- 1/4 cup strawberry jelly [50 ml]

**Cook:**

Beat 2 butters and brown sugar in cream.

Add the egg yolks and flour and mix well.

With a tablespoon, form small balls of 15 ml each.

Roll the egg whites into snow and roll each ball into the egg white.

Roll again in chopped walnuts.

Prepare a greased cookie sheet and place the balls and with your finger squeeze the center of each ball.

Bake at 350 degrees F. [180 C], 5 minutes.

Remove from the oven and make the cavity again with your finger.

Bake at 350 degrees F. [180 C], 10 minutes.

When the cookies are cooled, fill the center with 1 tsp strawberry jelly [2 ml].

# OAT-COCO Canna cookie

**Ingredients:**
- 1 cup soft butter [250 ml]
- 2 tsp coconut-canna oil [mixed with soft butter] [10 g]
- 3 cups brown sugar [750 ml]
- 2 eggs
- 1 tsp vanilla [5 ml]
- 2 cups sifted flour [500 ml]
- 1 tsp baking powder [5 ml]
- 1/2 tsp baking soda [2 ml]
- 1/2 tsp salt [2 ml]

- 1 cup coconut [250 ml]
- 2 cups of oatmeal [500 ml]

**Cook:**
Beat butters and coconut canna oil until creamy.
Add brown sugar, eggs and vanilla.
Sift together flour, baking powder, baking soda and salt.
Stir in coconut and oatmeal into dry ingredients.
Mix it all together.
Prepare a buttered cookie sheet or wax paper on the cookie plate.
Place the mixture in large tablespoonfuls on the cookie plate and flatten each biscuit with a fork.
Bake at 375 degrees F. [190 C] for 10 minutes.
Quantity: 3 dozen.

# OATMEAL & Raisins Canna cookies

**Ingredients:**
- 6 tablespoons fat [90 ml] (of your choice)
- 2 teaspoons of any canna oil (10 ml)
- 6 tbsp sugar [90 ml]
- 1 egg
- 1/2 cup molasses [125 ml]
- 1 cup all-purpose flour [250 ml]
- 1/2 tsp mixed spices [2 ml]
- 1/2 tsp salt [2 ml]
- 1/4 teaspoon nutmeg [1 ml]
- 1/4 tsp clove [I ml]
- 1/4 teaspoon baking soda [1 ml]
- 1 tsp baking powder [5 ml]
- 1 1/2 cups of oatmeal [375 ml]
- 1 cup grated carrots [250 ml]

- 1 tsp orange zest [5 ml]
- 1/2 cup raisins [125 ml]

**Cook:**
Beat the fat, oil and sugar into cream.
Stir in egg and molasses.
Sift together: flour, mixed spices, salt, nutmeg, cloves, baking soda and baking powder.
Add oatmeal to dry ingredients.
In the first mixture, add the grated carrots, orange zest and grapes.
Stir in dry ingredients.
On a greased baking sheet, drop by 25 ml spoonful.
Bake at 350 degrees F. [180 C] for 12 to 15 minutes.

# RAISINS cookies Canna

**Ingredients:**
- 1 egg
- 1/3 cup melted butter [75 ml]
- 2 tsp coconut-canna oil [mixed with butter]
- 1 cup brown sugar [250 ml]
- 2 tbsp milk [25 ml]
- 1/2 tsp baking soda [2 ml]
- 4 to 5 drops of vinegar
- 1 pinch ground clove [optional]
- 1 tsp cinnamon [5 ml]
- 1 cup raisins [250 ml]
- 1 1/2 cups flour [375 ml]

**Cook:**
Mix all ingredients well.
Spoon on to a buttered baking sheet.

Bake at 350 degrees F. [180 C], 15 minutes.

# PINEAPPLE Cookies Canna

**Ingredients:**
- 1/3 cup butter [75 ml]
- 1 teaspoon of your coconut-canna oil
- 1 egg
- 1/3 cup chopped walnuts [75 ml]
- 1/4 teaspoon baking soda [1.5 ml]
- 1/2 cup sugar [125 ml]
- 1/2 tsp crushed pineapple [125 ml]
- 1 1/4 cups flour [300 ml]

**Cook:**
Mix all the ingredients.
Spoon into greased sheet metal.
Bake at 375 degrees F [190 C] for 12 to 15 minutes.

# APPLE BISCUITS canna

**Ingredients:**
- 1/3 cup fat [75 ml]
- 2 tsp coconut-canna oil (30 ml) [mixed with fat]
- 2/3 cup sugar [150 ml]
- 2/3 cup applesauce [150 ml]
- 1 1/2 cups sifted flour [350 ml]
- 3/4 tsp baking soda [3 ml]
- 3/4 teaspoon cinnamon powder [3 ml]
- 1/2 tsp clove powder [2 ml]
- 1/2 tsp salt [2 ml]
- 1/3 cup chopped walnuts [75 ml]

- 1/3 cup raisins [75 ml]

**Cook:**
Beat all the fat, coconut-canna oil and sugar as a cream.
Stir in applesauce.
Mix dry ingredients: flour, baking soda, cinnamon, cloves and salt and to the mixture.
Stir in walnuts and raisins too.
Prepare a greased baking sheet and spoon the mixture on it.
Bake at 375 degrees F. [190 C], about 15 minutes.
Quantity: 2 dozen.

# BANANA BISCUITS canna

**Ingredients:**
- 1 cup soft butter [250 ml]
- 1 teaspoon of your canna oil
- 3/4 cup sugar [225 ml]
- 2 eggs
- 2 bananas
- 1/2 cup Carnation condensed milk [125 ml]
- 1 tbsp vinegar [15 ml]
- 1 tsp vanilla [5 ml]
- 2 2/3 cups flour [650 ml]
- 1 1/2 teaspoons baking soda [7 ml]
- 1/2 tsp salt [2 ml]
- 1/2 cup chopped walnuts [125 ml]

**Cook:**
Mix very well all ingredients and refrigerate for 1 hour.
Spoon on to greased baking sheet.
Bake at 375 degrees F [190 C], 15 minutes.

Icing:

- **6 tbsp butter [90 ml]**
- **1/2 cup brown sugar [125 ml]**
- **3 tbsp Carnation milk [40 ml]**
- **1/2 cup icing sugar [125 ml]**

Mix butter and brown sugar in a pot.
Boil for 1 minute.
Add condensed Carnation milk and icing sugar.
After mixing very well, spread over cooled cookies.

# Maple sugar ROLLS Canna

**Ingredients:**

- **2 cup flour [500 ml]**
- **1/4 cup baking powder [50 ml]**
- **3/4 tsp salt [3 ml]**
- **1/4 cup softened butter [50 ml]**
- **2 tsp canna butter [mixed with butter]**
- **2/3 cup milk [150 ml]**
- **1/2 cup maple sugar [125 ml]**
- **1/2 cup almonds [125 ml]**
- **Soft butter**

**Cook:**
Sift flour, baking powder and salt
Add the butter in small pieces and mix.
Add the milk and mix to obtain a soft paste to form into balls.
On a floured baking sheet, roll flat dough to 1 cm thick.
Brush the dough with mixed softened butter.
Sprinkle with maple sugar and almonds.
Roll like a rolled cake and cut into 2 cm-thick slices.

Prepare a buttered baking sheet and place the slices.
Brush each roll with softened butter.
Bake at 425 degrees F. [215 C], 20 minutes.

# DATES Bites Canna

Ingredients:
- 1/2 cup butter [125 ml]
- 1 teaspoon of your coconut canna oil (5 ml)
- 1 cup of finely chopped dates [250 ml]
- 2 eggs, beaten with a fork
- 1 cup sugar [250 ml]
- 1 cup Rice Krispies [250 ml] coconut to taste

Cook butter mixed with oil, dates, eggs and sugar over very low heat, stirring until thickened.
Cool for an hour and add Rice Krispies.
Using a small spoon, form a ball and roll in the coconut.

# PUMPKIN Cookies Canna

Ingredients:
- 1 1/2 cups sugar [341 g]
- 1/2 cup butter [114 g]
- 2 teaspoons of your canna oil (10 ml)
- 1 egg
- 1 1/2 cups cooked, crushed or canned pumpkin (341 g)
- 2 cups flour (454 g)
- 4 tsp baking powder (20 ml)
- 1/4 teaspoon nutmeg (1 ml)
- 1/4 tsp ground cloves (1 ml)
- 1/2 tsp ginger (3 ml)

- 1/2 tsp cinnamon (3 ml)
- 1/2 cup grapes (114 g)
- 1/2 cup chopped walnuts or pecans (114 g)
- 1 cup of bran or bran flakes (227 g)

**Cook:**

Mix the butter and sugar as a cream and beat the egg and pumpkin in it.

Combine flour, baking powder and spices and stir to make a paste, adding grapes, nuts and bran flakes while stirring.

Pour one teaspoon at a time of the mixture onto a cookie sheet leaving 2 inches of distance between each. (5 cm).

Bake at 375 degrees F (190 C) for 18 to 20 minutes or until browned.

Make about four dozen.

# RASPBERRIES Butter Canna

**Ingredients:**

- 1 1/2 cups fresh raspberries (375 ml)
- 1 tsp canna butter (mixed with butter) (5 g)
- 1 cup softened butter (250 ml)
- 1 cup icing sugar (250 ml)

**Cook:**

With an electric mixer, beat all the ingredients until softened.

Let it cool and spread, like butter, on toast, cookies, waffles or dry cakes.

# CINNAMON Cookies canna

Ingredients:
- 1 cup softened butter (227 g)
- 2 tsp canna butter (mixed with butter)
- 1 cup sugar (227 g)
- 1 separate egg
- 2 cups flour (454 g)
- 1 tbsp cinnamon (15 ml)
- Cut nuts or pecans.

**Cook:**
Mix the sugar with the cinnamon. (Keep some of it to sprinkle the cookies just before cooking in the oven.)
Mix the two butters, the sugar, some of the cinnamon and beat until fluffy, adding the egg yolk and mixing in the flour.
Stir into the unbeaten egg whites.
Pour in a cake pan or on a cookie sheet at least 1 inch of height (2.54 cm).
Sprinkle with walnuts and cinnamon sugar.
Bake at 350 degrees F (180 C) for 25 minutes or until lightly browned.
Cool slightly and cut into bars, while still warm.

Make about 3 dz.

# CHERRY Cookies Canna

Ingredients:
- 1 cup soft butter (250 ml)
- 3 tsp canna butter (15 g)
- 1 1/2 cups sugar (375 ml)

- **2 eggs**
- **2 tbsp milk (25 ml)**
- **1 tsp vanilla essence (5 ml)**
- **3 cups flour (750 ml)**
- **1 tsp baking powder (5 ml) (Chemical yeast)**
- **1 tsp soda (5 ml) (small cow on the can)**
- **1/2 tsp salt (3 ml)**
- **1/2 cup chopped cherries (pie cherries) (l25 ml)**
- **1 cup crushed cereal (Cornflakes) (250 ml)**
- **24 pitted pie cherries, halved**

**Cook:**

Mix both butters and sugar. Beat in eggs, milk and vanilla essence.

Add the flour, baking powder, soda and salt, mix well.

Add the chopped cherries.

Shape the dough (about, one tablespoon (15 ml) into balls and roll them into cornflake or other cereals.

Push one half a cherry into the center of the cookie.

Bake on a baking sheet, greased at 375 F (190 C) for about 10 to 12 minutes. Make about four dozen.

**Topping (Streusel):**

Mix in a medium bowl:

- **1 cup (250 ml) flour**
- **1/3 cup (75 ml) brown sugar**
- **1 tsp (5 ml) grated lemon peel**
- **1/4 cup (50 ml) softened butter.**

Mix well and spread on top of pie, cookies or cakes.

# Cinnamon apple and Cannabis delight

Ingredients:

- **2 cups applesauce (450 g)**
- **1/2 cup ground almonds (40 g)**
- **1 tablespoon lemon juice (15 ml)**
- **1 teaspoon cinnamon powder (5 g)**
- **2 tablespoons coconut oil (30 g) or add 2 tablespoons (30 ml) of Angel Cream or a few tins.**

A jam that can be used on toast, which is made with cannabis coconut oil having been decarboxylated before.

Mix 2 cups of apple butter, 1/2 cup of powdered or granulated almonds, 1 tablespoon of lemon or lime juice, 1 teaspoon of cinnamon powder and 2 tablespoons of coconut oil (30 g) or add 2 tablespoons (30 ml) of Angel Cream or a few tastes of tinctures. Mix the ingredients and cede them to a Mason jar and refrigerate.

# CHAPTER 11

# Hot and cold beverages

**DOSAGES, bail:**
Since it is impossible for us to know what intensities and qualities of cannabis you have in hand, it is also impossible for us to speculate on the dosage of your food? But, the quantities applied to each recipe, are only a suggestion, speculating that you use products of good quality and adequate intensity. So, as a matter of wisdom, be careful in your dosages and start by experimenting with small dosages of cannabis at once and progress little by little. But don't take the risk of cooking and ingesting garbage products from the black market. Unless insecticides and dubious mixtures make your trip… If you think it's OK for you, then smoke them, but don't destroy your stomach and immune system by eating or drinking it… Love life!

Liquids take you to a "High" faster.

## ANGELS' CREAM Canna
(Recipe into a Masson jar)
This delight is one of the best recipes to float quickly and cheerfully!

Ingredients:
- 2 ounces of marijuana (60 g) (all parts can be used)
- Hot Vodka (for its flavor)

- **Distilled water (so not to alter the taste of unwanted foreign minerals)**

**Emancipated directions:**

**(Step 1)**

Place (60 g) 2 ounces of marijuana in a jar (Masson jar) (all canna twigs can also be used).

Heat the mixed vodka (50/50) with distilled water, do not boil.

Completely cover the grass in the Masson jar with the heated vodka and distilled water (50/50). (Or a similar blend of pure grain spirits that you have in hand.)

Close the Masson jar and store it in a moderately warm place for at least 5 days.

Check occasionally to make sure the weed remains submerged.

**(Step 2)**

After five days, filter all liquid content into a high bottle that you keep separate.

In a clean Mason jar, soak the remaining wet cannabis residue in vodka, but without water.

Same as in the beginning, add vodka about an inch higher than the debris, tighten the cover and store for another 5 days.

**(Step 3)**

After five days, filter again the alcoholic liquid and combine it with the first liquid in your bottle.

Then, this time, in order to harvest the maximum of active and nutritious ingredients of cannabis residues that are still present, take the Masson pot and add only distilled water (no vodka) with your cannabis residues and let stand for another five days, you won't regret it.

**(Step 4)**

After 5 days elapsed (no more), loosen the cover and put the Mason jar and its content "45 minutes" in a pan of boiling water, but do not boil to a large broth.

Before putting it in boiling water, make sure the cover of the Masson pot is not tight, to let the pressure out.

After 45 minutes, filter the still hot liquid several times by changing the filter until the liquid is really clear of residue.

To complete it successfully, transfer the finished product with the other two extractions into the same bottle.


**(Step 5)**

Filter the three liquids combined again, to get the clearest drink possible, without floating particles.

But we'll probably have to rest the liquid for another week. This is why it is important to use a high bottle so that the residues are positioned at the bottom.

After a week, check to see if the liquid is clear enough for you, and siphon the clearest top and store it into a Mason jar with the cover loosen.

Place the Mason jar in a pan of hot water, bring over medium heat no more than 185 F (95 C) for 5 minutes.

Add a little honey to your liking, not too much. Mix well.

Transfer into a bottle, thin and high, and cap.

Leave to rest for a few months or more.

It doesn't take more than making your wine…

Make several bottles, but to convince you, taste this delight.

Go easy, you will feel the high in the next 15 minutes depending on your sensitivity; Be careful with that delight…

Always keep and rinse your filters and utensils and keep the precious liquid for your coffees, teas and soups.

Identify your bottles with the date, strength and name of the product. example:

- Cream of angels
- Today
- 45–65% tests

**Details:**
Many recipes require a double boiler. If you don't have a double boiler, use a larger saucepan and add a few inches of water that you heat up.

In a smaller cooking pot, which you add in the largest water, put your Masson pot after putting the recommended ingredients in it, such as the beginning of the recipe. Make sure the small cooking pot does not touch the bottom of the larger cooking pot directly so as not to risk overheating the underside of your grass. Put in the bottom, either a mesh or fill the bottom of Blanket Masson with the opening down, to make a kind of aeration layer. And if you're serious, shop in flea markets for a quality double boiler, but especially not aluminum. Do some research on the internet about the harmfulness of aluminum in your body…

# FLU & COLD Syrop Canna

From Grandma

Ingredients:

- 4 tbsp cognac (50 ml)
- 4 tbsp lemon or lime (50 ml)
- 4 tbsp honey (50 ml)
- 2 ounces glycerin (75 ml)
- 1 tsp canna coconut oil. (5 ml)

Mix glycerin with canna coco oil.

Thicken over very low heat.

Take as needed (hot)

And if you want more efficiency:

Marinate strong onions in apple cider vinegar and eat in two bite-sized bites 10 minutes before Grandma's syrup.

Cognac has a special effect, but if you don't have it, tequila, good brandy or good rum could do the trick.

Or, big Genova gin, the good widow safari, but you have to take it very hot and add 4 tsp of lemon or lime.

If your cold doesn't pass, then after a few shuts, you'll completely forget your cold…

# Fresh THC-Infused Coffee

**Recommended for starting the day pleasantly, but you must have the day ahead of you, as the recipe takes at least 50 minutes to brew and prepare. However, with the tinctures, 5 minutes.**

# Delicious Coffee Infused With THC

This coffee recipe takes far too long. It is presented for those who no longer have anything infused in hand. The ideal is to go through your dispensary and get a tincture or concentrated oil. You will then have your regular coffee, to your liking, with 2 drops and voila! Or you can taste it once you get to work, without the risk of driving…

**Ingredients:**
- **Coffee (depending on preference)**
- **3 cups of water (750 ml) (distilled water is always preferable)**
- **Your choice: butter or coconut oil mixed with 3 drops of tinctures or 1 teaspoon of your canna oil.**
- **The juice you harvest after an infusion recipe is ideal and can replace canna butter and other.**

**Cook:**

To start, granulate your weed as fine as possible with a good quality coffee grinder; a good result will depend on it.

As fast your cannabis is finely well granulated, heat the water (3 cups) (750 ml) over medium heat in a cooking pot and bring to a light boil.

Add your butter or coconut oil to boiling water to let them melt and keep over medium heat.

Butter or oil will help absorb cannabis as it boils slightly, allowing you to get your coffee strong later!

Sprinkle your ground cannabis on water and leave for about 35 to 40 minutes.

Stir from time to time, to allow your sprinkled cannabis to decarboxylate by mixing with oil or butter, because you already know that cannabis is not usually soluble with water, unless you have gone through various processes explained in this book.

To get a better result, it is best to use either canna butter or cannabis oil, but you will have a tasting with a very different taste.

Finally, the time elapsed, you have to filter the mixture through a small fine sieve and as soon as the precious liquid is passed to the filter, you are ready to prepare your coffee!

Grab your usual coffee, depending on the flavor or molding of your choice and add the recipe you've just made.

Of course you can then add other ingredients like sugar and cream depending on your taste.

**Note:**

If you need to taste quickly, without waiting for preparation or infusion, then opt for recipes with Cannamilk or other cannabis oils already decarboxylated. Also, to enjoy instantly: canna tinctures (if available in your country), or search the internet.

## Be Careful With Mixed Coffee and Cannabis

Be careful with mixed coffee and cannabis, as both have opposite effects; coffee is a stimulant, but cannabis is usually a soothing one. The result will depend on your digestive system and your predisposition to your body's reactions. The result could be that your effects are expressed only in the opposite direction to what you expected…

More information about cannabis-infused coffee, and teas, will be provided, read further.

When ingested, cannabis takes longer to take effect, more or less, depending on your digestive system. So if you're used to the quick effect like when you smoke it, expect it to be different. However, with the beverages, you will have to wait a little longer for the effects to be felt; however, your reward will be the duration of the effect, up to several times longer. But research brings new products to the market, such as concentrated tinctures, some of which take effect within 15 minutes. Or you don't have to go far, just try the Angels' Cream…

## Small recommendation for the refinement of taste:

Keep in mind that water from your tap that comes from the city or from your well contains unknown minerals that will transform the taste of your beverages. So don't trust any water that might contain minerals incompatible with yourself and also interfere in the taste of your tasting objects. So if you are serious with your wealth (your health) always use distilled water. (Minerals and vitamins can come from good fresh juices and vegetables and your fiber from your food.) If you are serious about your raw material (your health), you will live longer without serious illnesses…

# HOT drink cocoa kind

**Ingredients:**
- 1 pint (1.89 L) of almond milk or chocolate soy or half-half regular milk (your choice)
- 1 to 2 teaspoons cannabis tar (10 g) (or substitute for canna butter or tinctures)
- 2 to 4 teaspoons honey (10 g to 20 g)
- 1 teaspoon vanilla (5 ml)
- Whipped cream
- Salt or not (optional)

**Cook:**

Heat 1 pint of almond milk, or whole milk or half-half in a double boiler.

When the milk is hot, stir and mix 1 to 2 teaspoons of cannabis resin, 2 to 4 teaspoons of honey and 1 teaspoon of vanilla.

What you have on hand as cannabis is OK, but do dosage according to your absorption abilities. The preferences will always be the concentrates or coconut-canna oil.

Add a pinch of sea salt (optional.)

Whatever milk is used, you can also add 1 or 2 teaspoons of butter, to increase the fat content and help assimilate cannabis into your digestive system.

Serve in large cups with a spoonful of whipped cream to decorate.

The quantities specified of the ingredients are for 4 or 2 persons, depending on your desires.

All the ingredients can be according to your taste too, to experiment!

Serves: 4 servings.

# Canna latte with pumpkin and spices

**Ingredients:**
- 2 tablespoons pumpkin puree (30 g)
- 2 cup almond milk (500 ml)
- 1 teaspoon coconut-Cana oil (5 ml)
- 1/4 teaspoon vanilla extract (1.5 ml)
- 1/4 teaspoon pumpkin pie spices (1.5 g)
- 1 tablespoon brown sugar (15 g)
- 1 dosage of freshly prepared espresso

**Cook:**
In a medium pot, combine pumpkin puree, cannabis-infused milk, vanilla extract, pumpkin pie spices and sugar. Heat to medium heat and whisk constantly until steamed. Don't let the milk boil!

Once hot, remove the pan from the heat and reserve the milk mixture for later.

Prepare 1 or 2 strong espressos. Take the time to half fill your cups with cannabis-infused pumpkin spice milk.

Pour the espresso coffee into the milk and mix. Enjoy and adjust seasonings based on your personal preferences by adding sugar, a spice supplement or perhaps a little more coffee.

# Canna smoothie very refreshing
## coconut

The delight of a fruit smoothie, but with a touch of Cana with coconut.

**Ingredients:**

- 2 tablespoons canna butter oil (30 ml)
- 1 banana sliced
- 1 or 2 cup coconut milk (250 ml - 500 ml)
- 2 cups frozen or fresh strawberries (500 g)
- 4 tablespoons pomegranate juice (60 ml)
- 2 tablespoons pomegranate molasses, to sprinkle (30 ml)

**Cook:**

Heat the canna-coconut oil in a small pan.

Add the banana slices and cook for 3 to 5 minutes, stirring regularly.

Remove from heat and let it cool.

At the same time, put all your other ingredients in a blender, but without the pomegranate molasse

Add your banana, softened in the canna oil, to the blender and let the mixture stir, to a creamy look.

Make two servings, pour and taste after spraying pomegranate molasses.

Add ice cream to taste or experience your next smoothie.

Lick the precious juice, remaining in the bottom of the pan, with bread, you will have a tasting start…

Make 2 or 4 servings

# Lemonade Canna lemon, refreshing

Here's a recipe for a simple and strong marijuana lemonade using cannabis tinctures:

**Ingredients:**
- 6 cups of cold or water (hot to want to dilute faster) (1 1/2 L)
- 1 cup sugar (honey is better for your health) (250 ml)
- 2 cup lemon juice (about 8 to 10 lemons) (500 ml)
- 150 mg cannabis capsule or 8 drops of tinctures

**Cooking:**
Pour the lemon juice into your pitcher.

Add a kind of sugar to your liking and stir until completely dissolved. Hot water if you're in a hurry.

Add your cannabis tinctures and stir again. (You may substitute with 1 cup of Angels' Cream.)

Refrigerate for at least 2 hours and enjoy.

**Note:**
The strength of your tinctures may differ, otherwise dilute a little or let it rest by adding ice, as a precaution…

# CANNA Healthy TEAS

Cannabis is ideal for the consumption of choice, for many patients, as well as for pleasure. Some prefer a joint or a vaping, but cannabis tea is a hidden genius, which acts discreetly in depth, and which has survived for thousands of years…

Old countries such as China, India and Japan are millennia-old adherents and this practice is rooted in their genes.

Tea allows consumers to micro-administer as they want and to ingest their cannabinoid dosage more easily, discreetly and quickly, than other consumption methods. Some cannabis teas will be rich in THC or CBD, depending on the method of infusion and the product chosen. With legalization, concentrated products are becoming more and more affordable, and old methods of preparation through decarboxylations that are too long and burn some of the nutritional properties of cannabis will find less followers.

Consumers want to live fast, that's why the earth suffers. "No, not today, tomorrow we'll think about it! Today we have our tea in peace!"

You can take any tea or herbal recipe and easily add cannabis to the mix. Cannabis tea allows consumers to adjust dosages to their needs and consume discreetly in public.

Let's start from the fact that those who like to enjoy their tea or coffee, or other beverages, are not going to embark on big preparation ceremonies at all times of the day. We all know how to make teas and this book is not going to show you how to put one foot in front of the other, but here are some little-known suggestions to improve the healthy base, the water, for our teas, Canadians and Americans.

**Suggestions:**
1. Prepare your tea first, in distilled water (all city water or artesian wells have different tastes, because they contain additions of chlorine and unknown minerals, with which you may not be compatible). (Hospitals are not filled for any reason.)
2. Boil to a large boil, at least 3 minutes, pour into a teapot, let it stand for about twenty seconds to allow the heat to spread into the sides of the teapot; and there you insert your bags or your tea in bulk. (Loose tea for the connoisseur!)
3. Chamomiles or other flavors are your choice, the process is the same. (See other teas, below, you will find a wide variety of possibilities.)
4. After leaving to infuse for at least five minutes, remove the sachets, without pressing on the sachets, so as not to extract a pungent taste.
5. If you would do dosage before removing your sachets, then your sachets would leave off with plenty of your precious dosage of cannabis.
6. Then, only do dosage to your liking, with a few drops of tincture or concentrate that you have made yourself, according to recipes in this book.

7. Or, adding 2 tablespoons per cup of delicious liqueur: "the Angels' Cream," will make you dream "tea mentally…"

You may add your favorite additives, but the Angels' Cream already has its honey fermented with alcohol, in its composition…

- **Be careful with Angels' Cream, it's strong; wait 20 minutes and if not strong enough for you add some and remember the dosage for the next tea or coffee time.**

## TEAS that you can invent for your well-being

If you leave your health in the hands of your city that treats your water with so many products, it is you, with your body, who will pay later…

The ideal tea blends for hash smokers consist of a variety of substances: aromatic, soothing, or emollient, while being a healing agent and a mild astringent.

A mild expectorant can also be added, in addition to selected herb that will serve as antispasmodic.

## Several softening plants suggested for infusion are:

- **Anise and star anise**
- **Sassafras**
- **Red elm bark**
- **Tussilage**
- **Roots of comfrey**
- **Lin**
- **Licorice**
- **Marshmallow flowers, leaves and roots**
- **Honeysuckle flowers.**

## Soothing herbs for infusion are:

- Peppermint
- Green mint
- Thyme
- Sage
- Wood tea
- Cardamom seeds
- Girofle
- Cinnamon
- Jamaican pepper
- Eucalyptus, leaves
- Angelic Seeds
- Hysope
- Ginger root
- Coriander and catnip seeds.

When teas are infused with cinnamon powder, a gelatinous substance is released and gives the tea a viscous texture. But a small amount of the added raw cinnamon can be used as an emollient.

Marshmallow leaves produce less mucilage than roots, and flowers even less, but as said, never boil teas, infuse only. The same goes for licorice.

## Sweet astringent herbs, and also for infusion, are:

- Thyme
- Sage
- Rosemary
- Comfrey root and leaves
- Ginseng
- Aunée

For a pure intake of pure vitamin C, as a healing agent, with a tangy flavor like hibiscus are cannabis recipes suitable for the smoker, because tobacco burns vitamins C. Health stores and some pharmacies keep them in inventory, in powder form. It's a substitute for the famous lemon:

1/3 teaspoon is equivalent to 1,000 mg, but half a teaspoon is reasonable by adding honey if desired.

## Expectorant herbs are:

- Ballot
- Molina flowers
- Godard leaves
- Pulmonary
- "Forget-me-not," the leaves


Sage milk simply boiled in milk is popular in many Mediterranean countries and appreciated for its pleasant taste and especially for its favorable well-being on the respiratory system.

Hibiscus flowers are also beneficial for relieving coughs and inflammations of the throat. They are boiled in coconut milk, but cooled before serving as a much appreciated drink and also as a fancy drink.

In addition to being a good emollient, infused honeysuckle flowers also have antispasmodic properties.

To continue in teas in which you can add so many benefits, ginseng is an excellent tonic for nerves, blood circulation and glands. It also helps the body to pay itself and heal itself more quickly. Before a smoke laugh or a big canna-party weekend, foresight could avoid big headaches and sore throats; large dosages of ginseng root capsules or tea ginseng, ingested several hours in advance, and during the party could help get away with not too much damage.

# CHAPTER 12

# GUIDE: what the connoisseur can't ignore

## Too much cannabis edible?

### What if you've eaten too much of these delicious foods?

You may be affected while you learn not to eat too much while waiting for the climb. Maybe the dosage of the infused product you made your recipe with was too high? Maybe your injected products were mislabeled? The power and amounts you've ingested can make you fly too high, more "high" than you thought?

**But so far, research has shown that no one dies.**

### What to expect if you eat too much edible food

If you've eaten too much cannabis products and you are hovering too high, you're likely to experience an overdosage that's higher than your body could handle. You will experience a lot of discomfort, but less frightening than overdosage with strong drugs. Often it is only necessary to float while the aerobatics follow their course and let themselves slowly descend down under the clouds; but the aerobatics could last between 5 and 12 hours.

Based on lived experiences expressed by followers, you may experience paranoia, cold sweats, low blood sugar, panic, dizziness and worse, vomiting and a desire to sleep. Symptoms are experienced differently by everyone, but demonstrates that you need to eat properly and eat carefully.

## Calm Down Is One of the Savers

The THC, which is psychoactive, can affect you more. So start the evaporation process by:

- **Breathing deeply a lot of fresh air, especially outdoors, intensely.**
- **If you know of ways to meditate, it's time to make a comeback.**
- **If fear dominates you, then don't be afraid to consult a friend.**
- **If you think you have lost control, you can contact a health professional or a phone line for advice.**

## Reaching sweets (without canna)

You may have a rise in hypoglycemia or dehydration, so drink and eat anything that contains glucose, sweet juices, any sweets, sweet cakes; but absolutely nothing that contains cannabis. If it gets better. Keep filling your stomach.

## Chewing Some Pepper

Chewing pepper (the seasoning) can relieve it fairly quickly, depending on what "the victims of their delights" have experienced. The crisis of paranoia and anxiety has de-peppered as if by magic. Yes but do more:

- **Eating and drinking plenty of fluids**
**Fill in with lots of:**

- Liquids, juices, soups.
- Fiber food.
- Fat.
- And more sweets

A set of gestures can slow down the rate at which THC is absorbed into your digestive system and can help accelerate the effects of intoxication. As THC hides in your system, the effects are reduced as well. Many fatty foods can trap THC, while the fibers slow down digestion and pass directly into the large intestine to be evacuated. If you notice an improvement, then eat and drink water, again.

## Rest Obliges,
### In the Meantime, the Knowledge

If you have consumed CBD it is less severe than THC, because THC provides more very "high" high floating antic effects. Headache and red eyes will be part of it, so it's time to rest. The boss will understand that it is best not to see you at work with thick smoked glasses, especially on a cloudy day. It could take a few days off. Be Zen! And, let yourself recover slowly.

OK! It is said that the experience comes through our mistakes, so make sure you identify your products in order to understand how to do so, according to the intensity, which you are able to assimilate, and according to your sensitivity to the products you have cooked.

# No! Not the RED EYES!

## The Red Eyes and Marijuana
Many people who smoke grass has red eyes, WHY? This is caused by psychoactive components present in many varieties of (THC). Smoke a herb rich in THC, lowers blood pressure, which induces blood to the small veins of the eyes' white. The consumption of strong THC worsens this effect, which no one likes.

## How to Avoid Red Eyes
Many formulas have been developed to combat this effect. Among the miracle formulas stated by many, but which work, the ones mentioned here seem to have had good results. Above all it is prevention; then you will have to adapt one or more of the ways down here to avoid being told, "ha! You have red eyes, did you cry?"

## Have Eye Drops on Hand
A good brand of eye drops will be your choice, but just about anyone liquid that offers the possibility of relieving irritation, therefore, red eyes, should take effect and relieve your discomfort. If you wear contact lenses, you will have to give up and change to glasses, as eye specialists warn of the damage that could be caused by the use of certain eye drops, having been caused by cannabis smoke. Red eyes are apparently easily eliminated with eye drops, according to many users.

## Avoid, or Stay Away From Smoke
Smoke is not the main cause of red eyes, but added to many other factors, such as irritation if you smoke more often than in your turn. In this case, your tolerance to THC may be worth

reconsidering a break. You will need to quit smoking for a while to allow your body to eliminate overflow before developing an allergy. For a moment you might want to focus on softer CBD strains, ingested in your beverages and snacks of hot or refreshing treats or drinks. If not, then avoid by any means that the smoke rises in your eyes. Invent and think about improving your poor eyeballs…

As mentioned, CBD strains for medical or recreational purposes could be on your way out, to eyes back to normal and could at the same time prevent you from wearing sunglasses even at your inner work.

### Drinking water and more water

Cleaning your face with fresh water after smoking could surely help. Drinking plenty of water will help purge the entire system as well as the digestive system, moreover, could cooperate in regulating the pressure that causes red eyes. According to recent research, 75% of Americans live in a state of dehydration. The report specified that we should all drink at least 10 glasses of water a day so that our kidneys can do their job; to cleanse our bodies to keep it healthy with a good immune system.

Drinking water is also a good prevention but:

- **Breathing in large puffs of fresh air is also a good way to relieve the unpleasant symptoms of red eyes.**

# CBD for Chronic Stress, the Disease of the Century

The CBD helps millions of people with just about everything related to psychological and physical contradictions, including one of the discomforts of the century, the STRESS…

CBD to help combat chronic stress is quickly becoming available and appreciated treatment methods.

## The Enigma of Chronic Stress

While it is good to have a little stress to perform certain activities, chronic stress can cause a lot of damage, mentally and physically.

According to the American Institute of Stress, there are so many reasons why people are stressed. Some of the main causes are:

- **Increased workload**
- **Interpersonal issues in the couple and family**
- **Juggling work and personal lives**
- **Lack of job security**

On the other hand, lack of confidence in political systems around the world is also a source that exacerbates stress.

The American Psychological Association (APA) published a report in 2016 entitled: Stress in America, Dealing with Change: Which Analyzed the Different Causes of Stress in Americans.

## According to the results of their studies:

- **66% of Americans are stressed by the future of the nation.**
- **59% of Americans are stressed by potential terrorist attacks.**
- **61% of Americans are stressed by their financial situation.**

## What could be similar all over the world?

A survey released by the APA in August 2017, stipulated that 33% of Americans never discussed their stress management problems with their doctor.

Although stress may be a symptom of different diseases,

research is far from focused solely on stress. That's why it's important to see a doctor…

## CBD and research

- Epilepsy and certain neurological disorders.
- Depression and anxiety.
- Insomnia and sleep disorders.
- Treatments for cancer and cancer-related symptoms.
- Pain and inflammation.

From the U.S. National Institute of Health (NIH):

"CBD is an attractive cannabinoid with analgesics, anti-inflammatory, anti-neoplastic and chemo preventive activities."

- Diabetes and nerve pain related to diabetes.
- Cardiovascular disease.
- Arthritis.
- Muscle spasms.
- Multiple sclerosis.
- Post-traumatic stress disorder.
- Relieves stress.

For more details in the future, visit our blog: www.mari-juana-blog.com

# Jobs Requiring Drug Testing

You do not have the problem of passing a drug test if you know the type of job that requires a drug test. But many jobs require drug testing.

- The food industry
- Construction
- Education or in health care, your employer might require a drug test.

Often, a drug test for work is only a personal requirement of the person who owns the company. Some employers are more focused on efficiency at work than the kind of coffee they take to wake up…

## Whether or Not to Be Tested for Drugs

All workers in any type of job can be tested for drugs, even if you work in an industry that does not require it. Especially if there has been a stupid accident or bizarre behavior in the workplace. At some point, drug testing in the workplace is a matter of general behavior; according to statistics.

## Government Positions

If you work for the state or the federal government, you will probably need to take a drug test before or just after you are hired and even throughout your employment. Government jobs are among the most organized and consistent drug testers. Whether it's for an office or housekeeping job, if you're considering applying for a job in any government department, you should consider giving up cannabis.

But time is changing, perhaps in the future, public jobs will become a little less rigorous with drug testing. In the meantime, it's better to look elsewhere…

## Security jobs

Another type of work that requires drug testing at all levels is safety:

- **Police officers**
- **Prison Security guardians**

Private company security jobs also frequently require employees to be tested for drugs. Since it is difficult to know exactly what kind of drug circulates in the blood of the officer at work, speculation of the effects is open between paranoia, distraction and the likelihood of falling asleep at work. Cannabis is not really a stimulating media for this kind of work.

## Transportation jobs

Almost all jobs in the transportation sector require their employees to be tested for drugs:

- Truck drivers
- Bus drivers
- Boat captains
- Crane drivers
- Pilots, passengers or transport
- All jobs that require safe handling

Any other employment in transportation requires proof of sobriety, alcohol and drugs. Responsibilities to others are so tested on the road that the dangers of driving require perfect attention. Especially on the road, it is not recommended to drive while floating.

# How to Take Your Drug Test

If a scrupulous boss requires a tracking test for office position, then he exaggerates. You may have tasted good brownies the day before and not take the test the next morning. So we have to oppose, find an excuse and postpone the test until the next day.

Time doesn't change fast enough to take away the urge of a drunken boss to demand tests whether fair or not. So, what if you don't know how to prepare.

# There is a solution to everything

- First, stop drinking immediately.
- Drink plenty of water
- Do a lot of physical exercises to sweat and get cannabis out of your body.

- **And invest as soon as possible in a quality detox kit. (You'll find it on the internet).**

There is a solution to all situations and improvised drug testing is no exception. If your job requires a drug test, it would be a good plan to always have a good detox test on hand.

# CHAPTER 13

## Hemp and the planet "A"

Hemp, a variety of the same family as cannabis and a producer of CBD.

## Hemp clothing is growing in popularity!

While cooperating to save the planet "A" because we don't have a "B" planet.

## Planet "A" and Fast Fashion

Fast Fashion people are destroying the planet "A." If young people would refuse to wear fast fashion clothing, they would cooperate in pushing the fashion market to change clothing manufacturing materials and planets "A" would be wealthier.

## Hemp is a cannabis plant, like marijuana.

The two plants are related, like botanical cousins.

Trees, like hemp plants, fix carbon in our environment, unlike the industry that releases carbon dioxide into the atmosphere.

## Time changes, so we have to change too?

## Cotton production is not sustainable.

The majority of clothing is made of cotton, but hemp can be grown in half as much agricultural land and requires much less water, in addition to regenerating degraded land.

Hemp clothing is just one of the many uses of this plant. Hemp can also be used to make medicines, ropes, shoes, food and paper.

# Hemp Is From the Cannabis Family

When the word hemp is heard, we-all for a long time, think fishing nets, clothes, ropes and other fibers, but people never stopped thinking about cannabis. Yet, according to the memoirs of a Chinese emperor (2500 years BC), extolling the merits of hemp, the emperor "Shen Nung" published in his rich traditional pharmacopeia, the benefits of hemp.

Like the Chinese emperor, from the era before ours, hemp as a food had come a long way than clothing and ropes.

In addition, according to a 1997 discovery in the Czech Republic, clay fragments dating back more than 25,000 years contained fibers related to hemp and other wild plants.

## Hemp is now very prosperous.

The fashion comes back to hemp, as well as to hops, both of which are from the cannabis family and in addition, for one of these medicinal properties, CBD.

Some states have almost abolished prohibition, with limits, on age and a number of purchases. However, hemp is sold in bulk food markets across Canada and hemp is also mixed through granola with several other healthy seeds.

Due to the illegality of the cannabis plant at the federal level in the United States, the majority of hemp came from foreign sources (China, Canada and others), but everything is bound to change. The future of hemp rests largely on the (U.S. Farm Bill of December 2018) and how regulation will be expanded or limited.

# Hemp fibers are three times stronger than cotton.

They also retain their shape when wet, making hemp clothing less likely to stretch or lose shape over time.

It is also one of the fastest-drying natural fibers. Hemp remains extremely strong, even when wet. Thanks to its natural antibacterial properties (such as wool), you can wear them longer, before you need to wash.

**Hemp is also prized for its THERAPEUTIC CBD properties."**

# What is hemp oil?

Under the Hemp Industrial Agriculture Act, "what could change," hemp is defined as cannabis containing less than 0.3% THC. It doesn't say much.

Hemp oil is extracted from the seeds of the cannabis plant. The seeds are very low in cannabinoid concentrations, but very nutritious and tasty. They are high in protein, fat and fiber, but they are low in carbohydrates. But hemp seeds provide a reliable quality diet and a large amount of nutrients; this is one of the reasons why its attributes qualify, hemp oil, as a health product.

# The CBD hemp oil.

**To offer a better understanding of the use of hemp, it is worth mentioning the CBD hemp oil.**

CBD is the most common cannabinoid, apart from THC. While we have spent all this time growing cannabis plants to have high levels of THC, hemp plants have been grown to have a low THC content. Over time and through the selection of different plant varieties, this CBD concentration has become higher. Today, CBD hemp oil is extremely common and for many beneficial reasons.

# Beware of illegal markets

Our health is our main richness, so, you should require the source, written on the labels of your products, if the supplier is afraid to identify its source it looks like illegal markets…
Illegal markets are dangerous because they may contain carcinogenic pesticides that are harmful to health. Those who do not respect their bodies will never be able to count on anyone else to respect them better than themselves.

# Whole Thing Ready

The CBD hemp oil is already on the market; no preparation and here, in a few seconds a few drops in the morning coffee, on the other hand, do not use before driving. In addition, it will only take a little sun to brighten the day…

Some people take CBD hemp oil for its anti-anxiety and anti-inflammatory properties. All the reasons are good, especially since legalization, whose territories are expanding in the United States. In fact, many of these oils are already incorporated into edible food products, balms, ointments, lotions and bath oils. And the market is wide open for surprise… But the best way to fight against the black market is to cease fouling around with edibles to be sold exclusively in legal dispensaries. Edibles should be sold everywhere to compete with black market vendors who are everywhere…

# On the Agriculture Side

Known industrial hemp is of CBD content of about 1 to 5% CBD, but there are hemp genes up to 10–20% CBD. It is not easy to find a feminized hemp, seeds provider, of rich in CBD.

Male hemp seeds are not desirable, in order to have a rich CBD crop. For those who wish to engage in commercial hemp cultivation, search for a list of quality, CBD-rich genes, and ensure that the distributor is able to provide data, detailing the veracity of these seeds.

## The Genetics of CBD-Rich Hemp

Cannabis-derived CBD and hemp-derived CBD are very similar to those that tests positive results from cannabis. But the law in each state treats these two sources of CBD differently.

Cannabis-derived CBD must be sold at a licensed dispensary. For a product to be sold in a dispensary, it must comply with all state regulations regarding cannabis. What is good for the consumer is that cannabis-based products and cannabis derivatives must be tested in the laboratory, packaged in child-proof containers, must be monitored vigorously from the beginning of the plant and must be sold behind the counter and prescribed by connoisseurs.

Compared to CBD of less than 3% in Hemp THC, the cannabis-derived CBD is more concentrated with THC (over 3%) and is therefore considered a psychoactive product and is therefore classified in the same classification as regular THC. Consumers in illegalized states, obtain their CBD products from hemp known as "industrial hemp" and these products can be sold nationally over the age of 18.

## Hemp in construction and insulation.

Hemp is used to build houses. More and more eco-builders are using a building material derived from hemp fiber. (Hemp concrete houses are well insulated and, of course, energy efficient and carbon-neutral.)

# Hemp Saves the Planet "A"

As hemp grows, it absorbs carbon dioxide from the air, taking advantage of photosynthesis and converts that carbon into vigorously growing stems and leaves. According to some scientists, hemp farms can even store more carbon than forests. This reduces a significant amount of "greenhouse gases" of carbon dioxide in the atmosphere that warms the planet.

# Hemp Cultivation Regenerates Soil

Farmers can rehabilitate their degraded soils by growing hemp. To save soil damaged by intensive agriculture and chemical abuse, hemp has come its worth in Russia.

After the catastrophic nuclear accident at Chernobyl, which had contaminated the soil, everyone thought the soil would be contaminated forever, but hemp was successfully planted to restore the soil. The strong deep root structure of hemp and its tendency to grow rapidly and vigorously has been able to successfully remove toxins and heavy metals from the soil.

# Cotton (FF) Devours Tons of Water

The destructive clothes of (FF) Fast Fashion are unnatural, as much as sugar cane that pollutes the environment every time it burns. "And few people care."

My boat was on a slip in Indian Town Florida and when they are burning the sugar cane you should have seen the black dust coming from everywhere. Finally, I move out of there.

Cotton devours tones of water and chemicals, that abuse the soil by polluting it. Industrial cotton production is harmful to the environment, as well as to farmers. Hemp producers can

produce a ton of textiles using only half as much land as cotton producers. Hemp requires far fewer resources and can be grown extensively without too much water or fertilizer.
It is naturally resistant to pests and therefore does not require pesticides or insecticide.

# Canna Treats for Dogs

When human beings enhance their living, this is also the case for our pets. At last! Your dog can be relaxed and relaxed legally, in a much safer and more humane way!

Animal food producers have pushed the green revolution to the point of creating edible treats for dogs, based on CBD. Man's best friend will also be able to stray, alongside his master or mistress, from the human favorite plant. The point is that the "High" will not be for dogs. These pet cannabis products will not contain THC.
Do searches on the internet.

## Thought Sector

After a cardiac stop or a stay in the hospital, it's never too late to start exercising. Even though our heart is a good pump, it still needs our cooperation to help it circulate blood in all parts of the body. And nothing else, worth the regular exercise and even more, with water to help clean the junk food we ingest.

# CHAPTER 14

## Marijuana Vocabulary

### Marijuana

Marijuana, hash, hashish are all names given to cannabis which is a natural crop plant, of various varieties and which produces cannabinoids for multiple medical purposes and newly legalized for recreational in several states and countries. Cannabis has existed for millennia, but it is to be said: "who has therefore had the medical power strong enough to hide it all for so long from the whole world, the immeasurable natural possibilities of treating bodily abnormalities?" This was very similar to a global prohibition of the capitalist medical circle.

### Cannabinoids

Cannabinoids are part of the plant's basic genetic makeup, including a large number of different cannabinoids in the plant of different cannabis varieties. Different cannabinoids turn out to have a specific purpose. Human and animal bodies can benefit from cannabinoid receptors, thanks to their own system of endocannabinoids, which they naturally possess. The euphoric race towards the billions of dollars of cannabis has contributed to the deployment of research groups around the world; this led to the discovery of different cannabinoids for medical purposes. But let's face it, the therapeutic properties of cannabis and its derived varieties, such as hemp, and not to mention hops, which is also derived from the cannabis family; everything had been hidden from us since ever. Hops have been used in beer for a long time. According to old men, our pre-era ancestors knew and enjoyed cannabis-derived beverages.

## Endocannabinoid System

The endocannabinoid system is a system of cannabinoid receptors throughout our body and connected to the brain of almost all humans and animals. The receptors in the endocannabinoid system of each living being are individual as a fingerprint, which would be why each of us would react differently to each product of diverse strains.

## Indica

A cannabis variety generally described as calming and relaxing and may, in some people, cause drowsiness. It is differentiated by these compact and stocky leaves. Known varieties are: Hindu Kush, Nordel, Purple Chitral and so many others.

## Sativa

This variety is generally known as energizing and euphoric and it could give the impression of stimulating brain activity; it is distinguished by its slender and thin leaves. Known varieties are: Delahaze, Blue Dream, Maui Wowie and so many others. The race for the new names is triggered…

## Hybrid

The hybrid variety offers a mix of Sativa and Indica effects. It is such a name, a cross whose leaves are less stocky than the Indica and less slender than the Sativa. Famous varieties are: Banana Split, Lemon Skunk, Kali Mist, Sour Kush and so many others.

## THC

THC is the psychoactive cannabinoid that provides the consumer with a euphoric "High" which is one of the reasons that places THC, the best known and most abundant cannabinoid in most cannabis varieties. Especially because

THC has been shown to have great qualitative medicinal properties, whose primary medical goal would be to relieve chronic pain and stress and other related symptoms.

## CBD

CBD is the second most used cannabinoid. It is a non-psychoactive compound found in marijuana. CBD has the greatest medicinal value. It acts on the absorption of THC and the property of modulating its effects, including the unpleasant effects of paranoia and anxiety. CBD is now used to treat cancer, seizures, Alzheimer's disease, diabetes, gastrointestinal diseases, chronic pain and even skin conditions. CBD has changed the lives of many medical patients, and it is available in various forms.

### Terpenes

Each cannabis variety has different terpenes, it is the natural aroma present in all flowers and in all foods and also in cannabis. Some terpenes, based on lived experiences, would provide different high "highs". That's probably the deduction, or why? "There are so many expensive perfumes sold in fancy stores."

### Flower, Top, Bud

The flower is one of the terms used to describe the natural shape of the head of cannabis. The flower is the bud, the casserole, which consumers smoke most often. The flower comes from the very plant of cannabis, usually classified as Sativa or Indira. The flower is usually smoked in a joint, bowl or bang, but is recommended to obtain a quality THC in the decarboxylation process. Smoking of the flower remained one of the most popular methods of cannabis use, until the legalization and market entry, new products such as concentrates of 60% to 82%, oils, tinctures, concentrated waxes, bright resins, etc.

# Edibles

The term "edible," when it comes to cannabis, specifies, a food that is infused with THC or CBD. Edible products are usually a kind of treat, such as cookies, brownies, chocolate bars, gelatinous and also muffins. They are made by taking a concentrated form of THC and infuse it into food with butter or oil that has been decarboxylated from a cannabis product. Edibles require caution, because depending on the THC strength induced in butter or canna oil, they can be extremely powerful. When ingested, food is broken down by the digestive system, which according to the sensitivity of our endocannabinoid system, produces a compound that can be 10 to 20 times more psychoactive than smoking casseroles. The extreme high lasts several times more than smoking, there is the economy by the yield. Consumption is ideal for medications and also for non-smokers.

## Tinctures

Using a tincture is one of the fastest ways to get cannabis into your system. The tinctures are expensive, but if the calculation is made according to the power and speed of efficiency and especially the possibility of use without it smelling and it looks. Tinctures are an extremely concentrated form of THC or CBD; a bit like a liquid medicine that we add to our beverages or that we can also slip a drop under the tongue. Tincture is usually a mixture of CBD oil and essential oils for typical medicinal purposes. The CBD tinctures are favored by wealthier consumers…

## Topical

Markets flock lotions, ointments or balms that apply directly to the skin. These ointments are infused with THC or CBD to relieve pain or satisfaction in the applied parts. CBD-based lotions help treat a multitude of skin problems and sunburn. In addition to bio-gel typical that offers a relaxing and numbing sensation in muscle pain or for massages. This is just the beginning.

**Thought Sector**

New research has been said that marijuana is, since ever, naturally being part of us all, but we should realize that we are part of it.

Cannabis, known as marijuana was already used, thousands of years ago, in old countries and not to mention the old tribal remedies of the, not that far time, of the sorcerer's stories.

# CHAPTER 15

# Substitutions:

**FOR SUBSTITUTING ALIMENTS in your recipes, check the quantities.** Recipes come from all parts of the world and often with different terms:

**MILK PRODUCTS and egg products**

**Replace 1 cup of whole milk with:** 1/2 cup of evaporated milk plus 1/2 cup of water, or 1 cup of skimmed or reconstituted powdered milk, plus 2 teaspoons of butter or oil.

**Replace 1 cup of buttermilk or safe milk with:** 1 tablespoon of vinegar or lemon juice plus enough milk to make 1 cup and let stand for 5 minutes.

**Replace 1 cup of sour cream with:** 1 cup plain yogurt or 1 cup of evaporated milk plus 1 tablespoon of vinegar or 1 cup of cottage cheese blended with 2 tablespoons of milk and 1 tablespoon of lemon juice.

**Replace 1 cup of cream half and half with:** 7/8 cup of milk plus 3 tablespoons margarine or butter, or 1 cup of evaporated milk.

**Replace 1 cup of plain yogurt with:** 1 cup of safe milk or 1 cup of buttermilk.

**Replace 1 egg with:** liquid products sold as egg substitutes can sometimes be used, check the equivalencies on the package. But, for 1 egg, replace with 2 egg yolks if it's for cream and puddings. But for cookies and pastries replace 1 egg with 2 egg yolks plus 1 tbsp water.

**Replace light cream:** 7/8 cup of milk - 3 tablespoons butter.

**Replace 1 cup whipped cream:** 3/4 cup milk—1/3 cup butter.

**Replace 1 cup of clear sour cream with:** 2/3 cup sour milk and 1/3 cup of fat.

## Flavors:
## SEASONINGS, FINE HERBS, SPICES

**Replace 1 tbsp of freshly picked herbs with:** 1 tsp of the same dried herbs or 1/4 ground or powdered.

**Replace 1 tsp of poultry seasoning with:** 1/4 tsp thyme plus 3/4 tsp, sage.

**Replace 1 tsp pumpkin pie spice with:** 1/2 tsp cinnamon, 1/8 tsp ground Jamaican pepper, 1/8 tsp nutmeg and 1/2 tsp ginger.

**Replace 1 clove of garlic, finely chopped or pressed with:** 1/8 to 1/4 teaspoon dehydrated chopped garlic or 1/8 teaspoon garlic powder.

**Replace 1 medium onion with:** 2 tbsp dehydrated or finely chopped onion or flakes or 1 1/2 teaspoon onion powder.

**Replace 1 medium lemon with:** 2 to 3 tablespoons fresh juice.

**Replace 1 medium orange with:** 1/4 to 1/3 cup fresh or frozen or concentrated orange juice.

**Replace White Wine with:** An equivalent amount of apple or cider juice.

**Replace 1 cup of chicken or beef broth with:** 1 tsp instant broth or 1 cube of broth plus 1 cup of water.

**Replace 1 cup of honey:** 1 1/4 cups sugar—1/4 cups water

## Pastries:

**Replace 1 cup of flour prepared with:** 1 cup all-purpose flour + 1 1/2 teaspoons baking powder + 1/2 teaspoon salt.

**Replace 1 cup of cake flour with:** 7/8 cup sifted all-purpose flour.

**Replace 1 tsp baking powder with:**
1/4 teaspoon baking soda + 1/2 teaspoon cream of tartar.

**Replace 1 tbsp cornstarch with:** 2 tbsp flour.

**Replace 1 packet of active dry yeast with:** 1 tbsp dry yeast (chemical yeast).

**Replace 1/4 cup of fine breadcrumbs with:** 1/4 cup cracker crumbs or 1 slice of crumbled bread or 2/3 cup instant oatmeal.

**Replace 1/2 teaspoon of baking powder with:** 1 egg.

**Replace 1 cup of baking flour with:** 7/8 cup bread flour.

**Replace 1 cup of thick sour cream with:** 1/2 cup safe milk and 1/2 cup fat.

## The thickeners:

**Replace 1 tbsp cornstarch with:** 2 tbsp flour or 1 1/3 tablespoons fast-cooking tapioca.

**Replace 1 tbsp flour with:** 1 1/2 teaspoons cornstarch, or 2 tsp fast-cooked tapioca, or 2 egg yolks.

**Replace 1 tbsp tapioca with:** 1 1/2 tablespoons of all-purpose flour.

## CHOCOLAT, substitutions :

**Replace 1 square of semi-sweet chocolate with:** 1 square of unsweetened chocolate plus 1 tbsp sugar.

**Replace 1 square of unsweetened chocolate with:** 3 tbsp cocoa plus 1 tbsp fat or margarine.

**Replace 1/2 cup of semi-sweet chocolate chips with:** 3 squares of semi-sweet chocolate.

## Vegetables Substitutions:

**Replace 1 cup (250 ml) canned tomatoes with:** 1 1/3 (333 ml) fresh tomatoes, simmered for 10 minutes.

**Replace 1 cup (250 ml) of tomato sauce with:** 1 cup canned boiled tomatoes, in a blender or 1 cup seasoned tomato puree or 3/4 cup tomato puree plus 1/4 cup water.

**Replace 1 cup (250 ml) of tomato juice with:** 1 cup tomato sauce plus 1/2 cup water.

**Replace 1/2 cup (125 ml) of ketchup or chili sauce with:** 1/2 cup tomato sauce and 1 tablespoon vinegar plus 2 tablespoons sugar.

**Replace 1/2 lb (225 g) of fresh mushrooms with:** 4 oz (120 g) canned mushrooms.

**REPLACE 1 CUP OF BUTTER**

1 cup vegetable fat + 1/3 teaspoon salt

1 cup margarine

7/8 cup lard + 1/2 teaspoon salt

## REPLACE 1 CUP OF SUCRE

3/4 cup well-packaged brown sugar + 1/3 teaspoon bicarbonate.

1 cup molasses, reduce liquids by a quarter + 1/2 teaspoon of bicarbonate.

1 1/4 cup maple syrup halves liquids + 1/4 teaspoon of bicarbonate.

1 cup of corn syrup reduce the liquids by 1/3 + 1/8 teaspoon of bicarbonate.

## OTHER substitutions

**Replace 1/2 teaspoon of Jamaican pepper with:** 1/4 tsp clove and 1/4 teaspoon cinnamon.

**Replace, 1 cup tapioca with:** 3/4 cup tapioca fast cooking.

# Metric equivalents: solid = grams

| All-purpose flour | Butter or margarine |
|---|---|
| 1 cup - 115 grams | 1 cup - 225 grams |
| 1 tblsp - 12 grams | 1 tblsp - 15 grams |
| **Sugar** | **Sliced almonds** |
| 1 cup - 225 grams | 1 cup - 80 grams |
| 1 tbls - 15 grams | 1 tblsp - 5 grams |
| **Icing sugar** | **Whole almonds** |
| 1 cup - 150 grams | 1 cup - 170 grams |
| 1 tbls - 9 grams | 1 tblsp - 10 grams |
| **Light brown sugar** | **Shredded coconut** |
| 1 cup - 200 grams | 1 cup - 75 grams |
| 1 tblsp - 12 grams | 1 tables - 5 grams |
| **Cocoa** | **Rice** |
| 1 cup - 110 grams | 1 cup - 210 grams |
| 1 tblsp - 8 grams | 1 tblsp - 12 grams |

| LIQUID metric | SOLID metric |
|---|---|
| 1/8 tsp = 1/2 ml | 1/2 oz = 15 g |
| 1/4 tsp = 1 ml | 1 oz = 30 g |
| 1/2 tsp = 3 ml | 1/8 lb. = 55 g = 2 oz |
| 1 tsp = 5 ml | 1/4 lb. = 115 g = 4 oz |
| 1/4 tbsp = 4 ml | 1/3 lb. = 150 g |
| 1/2 tbsp = 8 ml | 3/8 lb. = 170 g |
| 1 tbsp = 15 ml | 1/2 lb. = 225 g = 8 oz |
| 1/8 cup 35 ml = 1 oz | 5/8 lb. = 285 g |
| 1/4 cup = 65 ml = 2 oz, | 2/3 lb. = 310 g |
| 1/3 cup = 85 ml | 3/4 lb. = 340 g |
| 3/8 cup = 95 ml = 3 oz | 7/8 lb. = 400 g |
| 1/2 cup = 125 ml = 4 oz, | 1 pound = 454 g = 16 oz |
| 5/8 cup = 160 ml = 5 oz | 2.2 lbs. = 1 kg |
| 2/3 cup = 170 ml | |
| 3/4 cup = 190 ml = 6 oz, | |
| 7/8 cup = 220 ml = 7 oz | |
| 1 cup = 250 ml = 8 oz, | |

**Note: Some measurements have been rounded slightly.**

| Fahrenheit | Celsius | France, EU |
|---|---|---|
| 150 F | = 70 C | = T/2 |
| 200 F | = 100 C | = T/3 |
| 250 F | = 120 C | = T/4 |
| 300 F | = 150 C | = T/5 |
| 350 F | = 180 C | = T/6 |
| 400 F | = 200 C | = T/7 |
| 450 F | = 230 C | = T/8 |
| 500 F | = 260 C | = T/9 |
| Broil | Grill | |

## Donate
## Only for encouragement
**If the content is useful for you.**

If you have obtained this book copy of:
**Cannabis Recipes and (2 in 1) Connoisseur's Guide**
for <u>free on the internet</u>, then it would be fair, if you wish, to donate a little, by my account to PayPal.

No amount is too small or too large, but you have to imagine how ungrateful it is to make books, it requires so much work!

And I know that you know too: Nothing is free, there is always someone who does the work…

To make a PayPal donation, you need to have internet access and then you Click here: www.jasselin.com (On top in the web site you'll see DONATE)

Then click to donate to:
gilles@jasselin.com
Please mention the title.

Thank you very much, we appreciate your encouragement.

Also visit our WEB website:
www.mari-juana-blog.com

PUBLISHER SINCE 1979

www.jasselin.com

## **<u>Notes:</u>**

Thank you,

www.ingramcontent.com/pod-product-compliance
Lightning Source LLC
Chambersburg PA
CBHW061724020426
42331CB00006B/1076